STEVEN BIALOSTOK

RAISING READERS

Helping Your Child to Literacy

PEGUIS PUBLISHERS
WINNIPEG CANADA

Printed and bound in Canada

96 97 98 6 5 4

Canadian Cataloguing in Publication Data

Bialostok, Steven, 1954–

    Raising readers

    Includes bibliographical references.
    ISBN 1-895411-37-8

1. Reading–Parent participation. 2. Children–Books and reading. I. Title.

Z1037.A1B52 1992 649'.58 C92-098043-0

Peguis Publishers Limited
100 – 318 McDermot Avenue
Winnipeg, MB R3A 0A2
Toll Free: 1-800-667-9673

This book is lovingly dedicated to the memory of my mother, Blanche Bialostok, a reading specialist who would not have agreed with a word in this book, but who would have insisted that everyone buy two copies.

Contents

Foreword

One of the fondest memories I have of my childhood is of the time set aside every evening when my mother read aloud to my siblings and myself. That was around the time of World War II, and the classic tales of the Brothers Grimm, Hans Christian Andersen, the Arabian Nights—along with countless folk tales—were *de rigeur*.

Sundays were especially exciting. On morning radio Uncle Don or some other celebrity would read "the funnies" while my brother and I followed along, as did millions of other American kids. Maggie and Jiggs, Joe Palooka, Prince Valiant, Alley Oop, the Katzenjammer Kids, Blondie and Dagwood, as well as the gang on Gasoline Alley, were as well known to me as Cinderella, Red Riding Hood, Sleeping Beauty, the Three Pigs, the Three Bears, the Three Billy Goats Gruff, and other familiar friends from literature.

And then on Sunday afternoons, the family would visit my Irish grandparents in the next town. There, my grandfather Tom would read the funnies aloud at *his* house. Every Sunday—a double whammy.

You can imagine how much I wanted to go to school and learn how to read! But that experience was a near disaster. Somehow the storylines of "see Dick run" and the beautiful Rapunzel (whose long hair formed the ladder that allowed first the wicked witch and then the handsome prince to reach her in the doorless castle tower) didn't have anything to do with one another. I opted for Rapunzel. Thank goodness the nightly story hour and, later on, library books kept my love of stories and books alive.

There's no guarantee that reading aloud to children will make them lifelong readers, but it seems to work with lots of kids. Besides, it's such an easy thing to do, it's certainly worth the try.

Steven Bialostok has made the try even easier with this book. Long a teacher of children, he gives parents a wonderfully clear road map to show them how to go about it. The examples of young people and their love of reading and of books will be inspiring to any parent or grandparent—even teachers!—and will make any adult want to try reading aloud to the young people in their lives.

Thanks, Steve!

Tomie dePaola
New Hampshire

Acknowledgments

While I would like to believe that brilliant insight came to me in a scholarly dream, I have been strongly influenced by a number of people.

This book is dedicated to the memory of my mother, but it would not have been written were it not for my early association with Robert and Marlene McCracken. They were my mentors and friends and I am grateful for all that they shared with me.

Dorothy Watson, professor of reading at the University of Missouri, took time to read my manuscript and offered many valuable suggestions.

It is said that only a handful of teachers ultimately influence our lives. Here is my handful: Drs. Madeline Bunning and Heath Lowry, University of the Pacific, believed in and encouraged me during my tumultuous first year of teaching. Lenore Bruckner, UCLA, always reassured me that my ideas about reading were important but reminded me that I must get older and hold an advanced degree before someone would listen. Ken and Yetta Goodman, University of Arizona, empowered, liberated, and continue to inspire me. Richard Dokey, my high school creative writing teacher, told me to write a book someday. And Richard Brown, my grade five teacher, was the one good thing I remember about elementary school.

There are also friends like Claire Rotolo, Charlotte Schell, and Judy Crocker who supported me during my early years of reading workshops as we frequently discussed many of the ideas presented in this book. Last, but not least, is Marcee Samberg, who, more than anyone, has watched me work with children, listened to my workshops, helped with the dishes, chopped the cilantro, helped me pack and repack my suitcases, talked with me about life into the wee hours of the morning, and spent endless hours editing this book in an attempt to eliminate all my preachy self-righteousness.

ONE

What This Book's About

As a teacher of young children, I have noticed that the controversy over how to teach reading in school comes second only to the controversy over sex education. Little else agitates a staff of elementary school teachers more than introducing a new reading series into the school. Nothing can alienate two normally friendly teachers more than if one of these teachers attends a reading workshop and is suddenly turned on to a new approach that the other teacher hates. Parents' concern over their child's reading ability (or lack of ability) will invariably bring them to the teacher's or principal's office demanding, "Why isn't our child reading at grade level?"

The parents' need to hear their child read his or her very first words can only be exacerbated by parking lot conversation (competition!) among the parents who drive the carpools. Usually reasonable and levelheaded, Gail is silently enraged when she hears how much "better" her neighbor's child is reading. "My son," says the neighbor to Gail, "has been in kindergarten for only two months, and he's already reading. They've put him in the top reading group!" Maria is dumbfounded when Sandy brags about her daughter Virginia. "She could read before she entered kindergarten," says Sandy. Maria is baffled when Sandy adds, "I'm just worried that she'll be bored in school." Cindy cowers when all these parents turn to her asking, "How's Billy doing?" In parentese, this question means "Is your child reading better or worse than my child?" Cindy feels compelled to consider hiring a private tutor for her Billy as he isn't reading yet.

Sometimes this conversation about reading extends well beyond the parking lot to dinner parties. Here, comfortable in their distance from the classroom, parents can carefully dissect the local schools and teachers. Says one parent: "Philip's teacher believes that children learn best through phonics. He brings a phonics workbook page home every night for homework." A second parent states: "My son's teacher is sending home sight-word cards for him to memorize. He has to know them all by next Friday." A third parent reluctantly confesses that her son's teacher ". . . doesn't really care if he can read. She just wants him to love school."

This introduction to your child's first schooling may not always be quite so competitive, consuming, or pressured, but these situations do exist. For many parents, a child's early reading can be a status symbol—like owning an expensive car. When their child is not as fluent a reader as hoped for, some parents develop a mental disorder referred to as "dyslexaphobia"—irrational fear of learning disabilities.

Few, if any, parents excuse their child's inability to read in the same way that they would excuse poor mathematical performance. "Oh," says one father, "I wasn't any good at math either." The moment his first-grade child shows signs of reading "below grade level" though, there are at least two parent-teacher conferences, a referral to the reading specialist, a battery of tests, and ultimately, a diagnostic label. Even parents whose child is reading "at grade level" can be overly concerned with their child's progress. These parents will often request their child's ranking in the classroom, "Is he [she] in the high, middle, or low group?"

Schools contribute to this high anxiety. Most parents are well aware of their child's reading level because the school is more than happy to reveal standardized test scores. Here, computerized results rank children locally, regionally, and nationally. These tests claim to analyze each child's strengths and weaknesses, and some even offer remediation techniques. Schools also place children into reading-ability groups, pull-out groups, or tracked groups in the classroom. Do you remember being one of the Bluebirds, the Pigeons, or the Turkeys?

Schools add further to parental confusion by changing reading programs as often as parents change children's diapers. Reading is a lot like fashion. One year something is popular and "in"; the next year it's "out." Even if a school keeps the same reading series, the publisher will certainly "revise and improve" it, necessitating the purchase of newer materials and books. Either scenario forces teachers who have never worked with a particular reading program to explain that program at "back-to-school night." This is difficult for the teacher, but even more difficult for the parents who discover that their child will be a guinea pig that year. "I'm just experimenting with this program now," says the teacher, "and I'm sure that I will be much more familiar with it next year." Imagine hearing your surgeon saying the same thing on the day of your coronary bypass.

Obviously, not all these scenarios occur all of the time. There are parents who maintain a calm wait-and-see attitude; there are parents who divorce themselves completely from their child's education; there are schools that are not fashion conscious; and there are teachers who can state—with much authority—the theoretical rationale behind their particular reading methodology.

But I fear the unfortunate examples occur more frequently than is good for our children.

Much is currently being said about reading aloud to children. Organizations use the media to extol the virtues of reading, encouraging children to read because it is good for them, and encouraging parents to read to their children because it is important. While these issues *are* important, no one ever tells parents specifically *why* reading aloud to their children is important; they talk only of the importance of developing positive attitudes about reading.

Also current is a growing educational movement— whole language—that emphasizes the use of children's literature as a method of teaching reading. This is a dramatic reversal of the methodology advocated when most of us were in school. Parents should understand the reading process in relation to this movement.

As a reading language arts specialist, I have many opportunities to address parent groups on how children learn to read. These groups include parents of preschool and elementary school children from a variety of socio-economic, racial, and cultural groups. All parent groups seem to share similar concerns: How do children begin to read? What is the value of reading aloud to children? What is the role of phonics in reading? Are reading workbooks helpful? What skills should children possess before entering kindergarten? What should parents do to prepare their children for kindergarten (or first grade, second grade . . .)? How do children become fluent readers? What can parents do with their children once they begin reading? If reading books aloud is so important, how can parents choose good children's books? What do you do when children ask to hear the same story again and again?

This book answers these questions by addressing your role—that of the parent—in the reading process. I will discuss how children develop literacy, and how reading aloud to your child (with the child's natural attention to a book's print), providing experiences for your child, and talking with your child are the most important causal factors in your child's learning to read. Similarly, by examining elementary school and classroom reading philosophies that build upon the parent's role as "literacy nurturer," you will be better equipped to identify and support these classrooms, and will never again underestimate your critical and determining role in your child's reading.

TWO
Why Do We Read?
We Read for Meaning

Forget the *hows* of learning to read for the moment. Assume reading is as involuntary as breathing, that no one has to learn how to do it. What, then, is its purpose? There is only one: *We read to get meaning.* If you read a novel, you gain meaning by appreciating the characters and following a plot. If you read a newspaper, you gain meaning by learning about the events of the day. If you read a textbook, you gain meaning by understanding factual information.

As you read this book, you will gain meaning too— about the reading process. While you are reading, you may not consciously think about what you are learning, but subconciously you know it. When reading any form of literature, every fluent reader knows, consciously or not, "I will get meaning from this."

Fluent and purposeful readers don't read to learn new words or to practice phonics, although there may be unfamiliar words or sounds in what is read. But the task is not to learn those words or sounds. The task is to get the meaning.

If getting meaning is what reading is all about, consider for a moment how you think you learned to read. I say "think" because how we think we learned to read and how we really learned are often quite different.

Many of my contemporaries were taught to read through the busy and fruitful lives of Dick and Jane. Their daily routines and conversation may still haunt you: "See Dick. See Jane. See Spot. Run, Dick. Run, Jane . . . Run, Spot."

While those who were taught to read using Dick and Jane books may remember reading them with some degree of baby boomer nostalgia, recall what occurred when we picked up our first Dick and Jane books. Each of our teachers probably wrote *see, run, fast,* and other words from the story on the chalkboard. They told us that these words appeared in our story. We tried to learn them through the use of flash cards. If we were lucky, we tried to learn the words through a game or two. After we learned the words—according to the theory—we would be able to read the story.

But what story? What could possibly be extrapolated from sentences like, "Run fast, Jane. Run fast, Dick." "Oh, Mother, Mother." There *was* no real story. There *was* no substantial plot. Whatever story existed resulted from the words the authors wanted children to learn.

Learning the words was more important than the story. Meaning—the purpose of reading—was secondary.

The response to Dick and Jane (and other sight-word programs) was teaching children to read through phonics. Many of you reading this book believe you were taught to read phonetically. The following is an excerpt from one of *your* stories: "The cat had a hat. The rat sat on the hat. The cat ran after the rat on the hat." Or, for the more advanced: "Bob had a dog and a cat. Bob's pets sat on the bus." The first line provides an example of a story written to focus on the "short *a*" sound. The second line extends the idea to other vowel sounds. Phonetic approaches require students to memorize sounds (consonants and vowels) and then blend them together to form words. Stories are concocted to reinforce the sounds already taught. Words cannot appear in these stories until the sounds of those particular words are taught. Comprehension questions and activities occur only after children learn to blend sounds. Once again, meaning is of secondary importance.

As with the Dick and Jane stories, "The Rat on the Hat" and "Bob's Dog and Cat" had nothing to say. There was no content. Even if meaning was of prime importance (which it was not), there was no meaning to get. These "stories" had no point. But why should they? They were not written to have meaning. They were not written to make sense. They were written to teach words and sounds.

Unfortunately, the ability to read is not automatic. But all children should learn to read. Publishers of reading programs bank on this and create various materials and texts to help teach children how to read. Even the most conservative educators today would not encourage the use of Dick and Jane. But reading programs that followed Dick and Jane have only updated the same idea: using stories created for the sole purpose of teaching words and/ or sounds.

Traditionally, these programs (and there are hundreds of them) came in two forms: sight word and phonetic. Both approaches ultimately served the same purpose: to teach children to state words. The sight-word programs required children to recognize whole words, and the phonetic programs required children to blend sounds into whole words. Some eclectic programs required both.

This is not to argue which approach worked best. Rather, the point is to emphasize the lack of consideration given to meaning. Meaning was placed in a position of secondary importance to—or at least in a separate category from—saying the words. Report cards, for example, often had at least two categories under the "Reading" heading: decoding (or word recognition) and comprehension. This implied that these two skills could function independently of each other.

Consider the following scenario:

Johnny enters first grade and must learn to read. He is introduced to reading through an approach that combines learning sight words and phonics. The teacher says that this is a well-rounded approach that will provide Johnny with the skills necessary to read independently. He spends the year memorizing the words (his parents help him at home every evening using flashcards), he practices blending his sounds (he is doing well in the middle reading group), and by the end of the school year Johnny is reading at "grade level."

Did Johnny ever learn the real purpose of reading—that you read to get meaning? Does he know that reading can be fun? He is probably so busy memorizing and sounding out words that he cannot even begin to fathom the greater depth of literature.

There are lots of Johnnies in our schools. Many children (even those identified as gifted children) do not understand the purpose of literature—of reading. My friend's ten-year-old nephew received a brand new book for his birthday. Opening it, the ten-year-old exclaimed,

"Oh, a book-report book." This child either did not know that books contain meaning or, somewhere along the educational line, lost faith in that fact. This child thought books were used to write reports. Second-graders were asked why people read. One responded, "To help people sound out words." Another responded, "To answer questions." A sixth-grader was asked the reason why an author had written a particular story. The child answered, "To teach me new words." In the corridors and classrooms of our schools you would be able to hear many equally frightening, sad, and not-uncommon responses from children. Many children think that the purpose of reading is to write book reports, answer questions, read flash cards, learn words, please parents, and please teachers.

The very first thing children must understand about reading is that books contain meanings, and that the point of reading is to get those meanings. In the process of reading, we may gain knowledge, have fun, become ecstatic, feel repulsed, be frightened, or even laugh aloud. But these are all a result of knowing that a message (or messages) exists in written material, and that one's purpose as a reader is to make sense of that message. A young child sitting in a parent's lap waiting to hear a ghost story grows excited in anticipation. Part of that anticipation is the knowledge that "Oh boy, my dad [mom] is going to read me a story and there's something in it that's going to scare the pants off me!" No child I know thinks, "Oh boy, my dad [mom] is going to read me a story so I can learn brand new vocabulary words." Unless a young child appreciates the basic fact that the purpose of reading is to get meaning, the rest of learning to read is pointless. You might as well give the child a book in a foreign language.

The best way for children to learn that the purpose of reading is for meaning is by being read to from the time they are infants. Being read to does far more than develop positive attitudes about books and reading (which it does, of course, and which should not be minimized). A parent reading aloud to a child does not care about teaching vocabulary words or phonetics. Reading aloud sends the critical message to children that books have ideas, and that the purpose of reading is to get those ideas.

Books are a form of language, and people respond to books in the same manner that they respond to oral language—by attending to the meaning.

When a newborn infant is learning to understand and communicate, the child focuses only on meaning, on making sense. The infant does not respond or memorize individual words or sounds before communication exists. When an infant hears a parent speaking, the child associates the words with ideas, not verbs and nouns. Two-year-old Josh hears his mother ask, "Josh, would you like some milk for breakfast?" Josh does not pay attention to individual words like *would, for, some,* or even *milk* before replying, "Yes, in my special cup." Josh cares about the meaning—about getting the idea. If Josh paid attention to the individual words or the sounds, he would miss the meaning.

This is how all humans learn to understand and communicate. They listen to language and respond to its meanings. I have never met parents who spoke to their child phonetically (*m-o-m-m-y*), or who used isolated words when speaking. We don't say "Cookie? Cookie? Good! Good!" unless we want to sound like Johnny Weismuller. We say to a child, "Do you want a cookie?"

without caring if the child understands every word. Similarly, when children attempt speech, the individual words that they use imply much more meaning than is inherent in those words. "Mommy" never means just the noun for mother; "Mommy" means any number of different ideas depending on the context in which the word was said. "Mommy" can mean "I am wet . . . I am hungry . . . I want you to hold me . . . I am frightened . . . I love you."

Children eventually speak using whole sentences. To do this they use complex rules of grammar, individual words and sounds. But they don't care one bit about this. Nor do we care about the parts of language as adults unless we are studying linguistics. We *do* care about meaningful communication, and we notice grammatical or phonetic distortions only when they significantly disrupt our understanding.

Children discover this by hearing language spoken. Children discover the same about reading by hearing books read aloud.

Children who are read to know without question that their first task is to understand, to get a message. For these children, there *is* no other purpose in reading.

With all the criticism of television today, we can be assured of at least one thing: Children who watch television know that the shows contain meaning. They know that their favorite show has ideas, and that the viewer's job is to understand the ideas being presented. No one has to teach this concept. There are no comprehension questions at the end of a TV show. (If there were, this might help to discourage television watching.) Children know that there is a story to watch, and that they must pay attention to find out what the story is about. Children do not have to analyze each frame of a television show to know what is happening. They watch the whole story and discover meaning and sense from it.

This is all to emphasize one primary reason why you should read to your child: to show that books have meaning.

If you already read aloud to your child, you deserve a pat on the back and encouragement to continue doing so until your son or daughter says, "Pu-leeze, not while my date's here!" Children need to continually rediscover that books contain meaning.

If a teacher (or a series of teachers) emphasizes learning skills rather than obtaining meaning, a child may become focused on those skills and ignore the real purpose of reading. This is particularly true as children enter second, third, or fourth grades (and beyond), in which more sophisticated literature is read and an increasing number of skills are to be taught. Meaning, unfortunately, becomes less and less a concern. Continued reading aloud maintains the integrity of reading, even in the midst of educational calamity.

If the time you spend reading to your child is minimal, because you expect the school to assume that responsibility, tch, tch, tch. Guilt, guilt, guilt! You are diminishing your substantial influence and importance in establishing your child's reading process. A school cannot possibly replace or duplicate what you can provide for your child in the first years of that child's life. Schools are filled with children whose parents have assumed that they played no role in preparing their children for reading. This situation is akin to patients who go to the doctor asking to be cured of illnesses that could have been prevented by proper health practices.

A doctor can only do so much if you don't care for yourself. A dentist can't guarantee teeth into old age unless you brush and floss regularly. A therapist cannot undo a miserable childhood.

A teacher, no matter how skilled, loving, hardworking, and devoted, cannot provide the groundwork that parents can provide their child.

Reading aloud to your child is incredibly important!

THREE
Prediction Through Experience

My friend Gloria and I were driving through the foothills one day when we decided that it was time for lunch. It was a warm afternoon, and we both wanted a couple of sandwiches. As we searched for a place to eat, Gloria noticed that there was a food stand across the field. I couldn't see the stand and asked her where she was pointing. Gloria told me that it was under a large Budweiser sign. I looked over to where she pointed but couldn't see a Budweiser sign anywhere. She pointed again saying crossly, "Right over there." Once again I told her that I didn't see this sign, and once again she tried to point the sign out to me. Finally I turned to Gloria and asked, "Do you mean the sign that says 'Michelob'?" Gloria looked, paused, and then replied meekly, "Oh . . . Yeah."

Before comparing the words *Michelob* and *Budweiser,* let me assure you that they are not alike. While both words have almost the same number of letters, the only real similarity between Michelob and Budweiser is that they both mean "beer."

A fluent and avid reader like Gloria really has no trouble distinguishing words. To understand her response, we must expand upon the idea of reading for meaning. In the previous chapter, the discussion of meaning dealt primarily with the author's ideas being conveyed to the reader. Reading isn't quite that simple. The author may have ideas to convey, but the reader brings to any piece of literature all of his or her life experiences and understanding of that subject matter. This personal background affects the understanding of that literature. That is why it is senseless to ask any person to tell you the main idea of a story. The main idea of any story is dependent upon the experiences, values, and attitudes of the reader.

When my friend and I watch the movie *The Wizard of Oz,* we differ on the major theme. I believe that the movie is about not needing to leave home in order to grow up. My friend, an analytic psychotherapist, believes that the movie's message is how individuals can grow and change through the use of group psychotherapy. (He believes that Dorothy, the Scarecrow, the Tin Woodsman, and the Lion could not get what they wanted individually but only as they grew together. The wizard, naturally, is a symbol for the therapist.) Some of you may scoff at my friend's interpretation (as I do), but is anyone more correct? What *is* the main idea of *The Wizard of Oz?* Some may agree with my interpretation, some may agree with my friend's, some may conclude that it's better to stay away from glass windows during a tornado, and some may see no meaning whatsoever. Each of you has your own idea of what the movie is or is not about, based on your background and experiences.

This is true whether you see a movie, look at a painting, listen to music, or read a book. The mind is not like a photograph that replicates what we see. The mind acts more like the visual image on an artist's canvas—one person's interpretation based upon his or her own background. No two people have exactly the same understanding of a movie or the main idea of a book. *Getting* meaning also involves *giving* meaning. My friend Judy, an artist, will never tell me what one of her paintings "means" when I ask. She always responds, "What does it mean to *you?*"

I have certain messages I want to convey in this book, but I have only a certain amount of control. Each of you reading this brings your own background to the text and interprets it accordingly. Meaning is a two-way street.

This concept is important to fully appreciate Gloria's misreading of the Budweiser sign. One's perception of print is strongly influenced by personal experiences and knowledge. You may think that when you read you pay attention to the print, but your personal experiences have a tremendous impact upon your ability to make sense from that print. Gloria misread "Michelob" because Gloria's perception of beer is "Budweiser."

The importance of experience to reading can be demonstrated by several examples.

XOXOXOXOXOXOXOXOXOXOXOXOXO

How did you read this? Some read it as the symbols used to play tic-tac-toe. Some see a pattern of Xs and Os. Many read it as the ending of a letter where these symbols mean "hugs and kisses." Perhaps you thought of something else. Whatever your response, your interpretation of these symbols originated from your experiences and not from the letters themselves. If you've never played tic-tac-toe, chances are unlikely that this would be your response. Unless you are familiar with letters ending with XO, it is unlikely that you would read this as "hugs and kisses."

Meaning is the result of experiences. The experiences we bring to print are major factors in our ability to read meaningfully—and thus fluently.

*P 3, SL next 2 STS to cable needle and hold in front,
k 2, k 2 from cable needle, rep from *, end P3.

Some of you can read the above passage and some of you cannot. For those of you (like myself) who have no idea what this represents, these are knitting directions. I have never knitted, nor have I thoughtfully observed anyone else knitting. Therefore, I have little, if any, information inside my head that I can bring *to* this "literature." I can sound out words or state words that I recognize, but the content makes no sense to me.

Those who can read the passage above understand the words, the abbreviations, and—if asked to read them orally—can do so with ease. Anyone capable of reading— and understanding—this has had experience knitting long before seeing knitting directions, knows what is supposed to occur while knitting, and has developed the appropriate knitting language.

Fluent readers of this passage bring their experience and their knowledge of "knitting language" to the same passage that I was unable to read. The difference between us is not the fluent readers' greater intelligence, their greater vocabulary, or their greater facility in phonics; the factors determining who can read the directions with a greater degree of understanding and fluency are the amount of experience brought to this print and the amount of visual focus given to the print itself.

I have no experience knitting and must therefore focus entirely on the print. Those who were able to read the directions have much experience knitting and could focus much less on the print. They were reading; I was stating words. There is a monumental difference between reading and stating words.

"Reading" involves immediate comprehension and fluency resulting from prior experiences with, and understanding of, the subject. "Stating words" does not require comprehension and obviously does not require prior understanding. Whenever we focus on stating words, experiences and comprehension are secondary. All the phonics and sight-word vocabulary in the world cannot help you read these directions if you've had no prior experiences. It would be much more valuable to give you the experiences first.

Consider the following directions I received for installing my ski rack:

1. Slide a weld nut inside a center post on a final assembly so that the hole in the center post lines up with the hole in the weld nut. Put a flast washer on a hex head screw and thread into weld nut loosely through hole in center post. Repeat on remaining three final assemblies.
2. Turn final assembly upside down and slide the inner slide (also inverted) into it, making sure that the weld nut enters the slide. Repeat on remaining final assemblies.

I never made it to #3. I paid the ski shop employee ten dollars to do it for me, and I have never taken the ski rack off the car.

The directions made no sense to me since I had no experience with the parts used or the assembly of something like this. Watching the guy in the ski shop put it together was helpful in understanding the directions; installing several ski racks with someone as I read the directions would practically guarantee my ability to understand these or similar directions.

The same holds true for my computer manual. When I first took delivery, I had almost no knowledge of the computer and could do little other than type. I didn't know how to set margins, tabs, columns, and so on. Reading the computer manual served little purpose until I had a personal computer tutorial. Now the manual is clearer.

The directions for assembling a child's new toy make more sense after you have assembled it. The map is easier to read if you've already traveled in that particular region and have some familiarity with it. The high school or college chemistry text is much more readable after you've completed the experiments and had the resulting discussion. When reading a text, the student can rely on his prior experiences to make the text simpler and predictable since meaning is now stored in his or her head and can be brought to the printed word. (Unfortunately, teachers usually assign reading the text as the first activity of an assignment.)

Our life experiences allow us to make predictions as we read. A prediction is an informed guess.

Unless you can predict much of the text before seeing the words themselves, reading becomes a laborious process of stating individual words and sounds. Fluent readers—both adults and children—have a strong sense of how the sentence should read even before they see the words. They know what makes sense. The more understanding the reader has of what is to be read, the easier it is to make predictions. The reader predicts the text as it is read by eliminating unlikely possibilities.

The fluent reader's only focus is on getting the meaning from the text and, usually without thinking, logically predicting what something *should* say based upon whatever personal information he or she already possesses. Seeing the words acts to *confirm* our predictions; it doesn't precede them.

Even fluent readers have more trouble reading text when they have little prior experience or knowledge of the subject. The text makes less sense. The readers cannot make predictions. The words suddenly become more important than the meanings they convey, as they do with most poor readers.

Even our best readers make numerous errors while reading. Those errors, however, do not distract the reader. They don't interfere with the meaning of the story. The errors are usually sensible ones; the reader may substitute a more familiar or meaningful word unwittingly or deliberately, because it makes sense. Fluent readers also skip words they don't recognize because they can get the meaning without them. They predict sensibly and get meaning based on what they know should make sense.

Obviously we must look at print to help us read. If we are blindfolded (and unable to read braille), we cannot read. But, in learning to read fluently, there must be a careful balance between focusing on the print and predicting (based on our experiences).

Since making predictions based on experiences is a major key to reading, providing your child with those experiences is an important parental responsibility. Experiences provoke thinking and language—the real "readiness skills" your child needs before entering kindergarten. Experiences allow print to make sense.

Important experiences aren't necessarily the trips to Europe, to the mountains, or even to the fire station. While these are nice, the experiences we provide children in everyday life are every bit as important and meaningful to children as the grand ones—if not more so. Walks to the park, trips to the grocery store, talks about things around the house, running of errands, and play with children are all important experiences. *They are significantly more important than letter or word recognition could ever be at the beginning-reading level.*

Experiences are the foundation for reading. No one else can provide these kinds of experiences as early or as significantly in your child's life as you, the parents. Don't minimize your importance here. And providing your child with experiences must not stop once a child learns to read, either. Direct experiences are just as important when your child gets older. They provide the information necessary for reading to make sense. (This, by the way, is one of the major purposes behind many school field trips. There is no better way for your child to obtain direct experiences than by actually visiting and becoming actively involved in something being studied.)

When reading to your child, or when your child begins to read independently and comes to unknown words, he or she should be encouraged to guess what those words are rather than being asked to sound them out. Children, often through inappropriate teaching, get overly involved in figuring out what a word says. "Sound it out" echoes in the brains of too many children.

Guessing based on what makes sense should be encouraged, not discouraged; it is the very essence of fluent reading. Guessing is essential for reading to occur. Guessing indicates a child's desire to make sense out of the words—out of a story or text or poem. When your child asks you what a word is, you might cover it up and ask,

"What do you think it might say?" If your child predicts incorrectly, decide if the prediction makes sense. If the child has been making sense out of the story to this point, the prediction will probably be reasonable—or at least accurate enough. And, if by chance it is not, a non-threatening question such as "Does that make sense?" keeps the focus on meaning. The emphasis must be on approximation, not exactness. Chances are that even if the guess doesn't make sense, further reading will result in a self-correction of the mistake.

Titles of books, chapter titles, and illustrations (especially on the book cover) also allow children to make predictions. Before beginning a book, you can talk with your child about the title, what he or she thinks will happen in the book, what the pictures tell the child about the story, what the chapter title implies will be occurring. This kind of thinking encourages children to predict what may happen in exactly the same way that reading the title of this book made you predict what it might be about. (No one begins reading a book if completely unfamiliar with its contents. Adults, too, use cover illustrations, cover flap summaries, titles, reviews, discussions with friends, and movies the book was originally based upon to help predict a book's contents and then decide whether they wish to read the book.)

Let me clarify that I am not encouraging following a "reading readiness" program with your child. Parents can be so deeply concerned with their child's education and take everything so much to heart that they forget the pleasure that these experiences bring. It's supposed to be fun. If you agonize too much (Am I giving my child enough experiences? Is my child predicting appropriately? Does my child pay too much attention—or not enough attention—to the print? and so on), you may be suffering from the social disease: over-involved parenting. Don't worry. It's not terminal. The remedy is to relax!

FOUR

Prediction and the Sounds of Language

I have said that all of us make predictions based on prior knowledge and experience. If the reader's predictions are valid, those predictions will be confirmed by further reading. While it is extremely valuable to have prior experiences with the subject matter of what we read (in order to make predictions), this cannot always be the case. Therefore, a second factor of equal value for making predictions comes from knowing how written language sounds.

Every fluent reader intuitively understands how books sound because he or she has heard books read aloud so many times. Let's try an experiment. Read the following passage:

The Boat in the Basement

A woman was building a boat in her basement when she finished the the boot she discovered that it was too big to go though the door. So he had to take the boat a part to get it out. She should of planned ahead.

(*From F. V. Gollasch, Ph.D. diss., U. of Arizona, 1980.*)

I frequently show this passage to groups of adults. Not one adult has read it "incorrectly." That is, everyone reads the passage so that it makes sense and—unwittingly—

27

ignores the printed errors, as many of you may also have done. Here is the passage again with the errors marked:

A woman was building a boat in her basement [*no period*] when [*no capital* w] she finished the the [*a second* the] boot [*should be* boat] she discovered that it was too big to go though [*should read* through] the door. So he [she] had to take the boat a part [apart] to get it out. She should of [have] planned ahead.

Undoubtedly, when you read this the first time, you—unthinkingly—made the corrections. We are all so familiar with how written language must appear and sound that we unconsciously made the corrections so that the passage made sense.

Our understanding of written language is so intuitive that while we read we sense what the words must say even before we see the print (just as in listening we can often predict what the speaker will say before we hear the actual words). We make predictions based on our knowledge of how language is constructed. Seeing the words acts to confirm our predictions.

I have been careful to refer to the importance of "written language," not just "language." Our knowledge of how written language works is only partially the result of understanding oral language. While written and oral language share the same vocabulary and grammar, written language does not replicate oral language. If children are to make predictions while reading (based on the sound of written language), they must understand the similarities and differences between the two.

Children must understand exactly what a written word *is*. Oral language has no spaces between the words. When speaking with each other we don't see where words begin and end. But there are spaces between words in written language. Many young children think "How are you?" or "Once upon a time" is one word; many think "Halloween" is three. Children who don't know what a written word is frequently become confused about print. They may confuse words and letters. They may not know what to look at on the page.

Children must also understand the direction of written language. Oral language has no left to right orientation. They must know the direction of written sentences. We can't speak in the wrong direction, but we can surely read in the wrong direction.

Children must understand the sound of written language. Written language sounds different than oral language. I have not in recent memory started a conversation with "Once upon a time" even though it is a familiar structure of fairy tales. If Dickens's *A Tale of Two Cities* was written to sound like oral language, instead of beginning with "It was the best of times, it was the worst of times," it might read "I've had mixed feelings about the past several years. Part of it was okay, but part of it stunk!" If I listen to the radio, I am fairly certain when the radio announcer is reading from a prepared script or speaking extemporaneously, even without the "uhs" and "ers." Even informal correspondence, which sounds conversational, is usually more precise than speech.

A final difference between written and oral language results from the context in which the two originate. Oral language relies not only upon words to communicate meaning but upon the entire context of the discussion. When two people have a conversation, much of the communication comes from other cues occurring at the time: eye contact (or lack of it), body language, the sound and intonation of the voice, and the degree to which each person understands (or misunderstands) the other.

Proper communication also depends on the context in which this communication takes place. When speaking to a group, I must know who my audience is, whether they are parents, teachers, or administrators. I must know if the audience has heard me before and what kind of background they have on the subject.

There is an understanding that occurs prior to, and during, oral communication that cannot occur as completely with written communication. As I write this, I can make only general assumptions about the audience of readers. Even though I have tailored this book for a specific market (parents of young children), my communication with you in this book is different than if I spoke with you personally. Since you cannot see my face or hear my voice, you must rely totally upon the text and your own background for understanding. In writing this book, I must write carefully and specifically for communication to be effective. (I have, in fact, rewritten this paragraph at least fifteen times to make my point, eliminating jokes and asides that would only be appropriate if I were speaking to you personally.)

There are also similarities between written and oral language that children must understand.

Oral and written language share a common vocabulary. Having a rich vocabulary makes prediction easier. A child cannot possibly guess what a certain word will be if it is not in his or her vocabulary.

Consider the following sentence: *Judaism is a monotheistic religion.* Unless *monotheistic* is part of your vocabulary, understanding this word is impossible. The word—

and therefore the sentence—would make no sense to you even if it were completely phonetic. However, if the meaning of the word *monotheistic* were already familiar to you, you would understand the meaning of the sentence.

Oral and written language share a similar grammatical structure, a structure that allows us to predict while reading. If I am reading the sentence "*The cat was on the* _____ " I do not need to look at the next word to know it must be a noun. It can't be a verb (*The cat is on the is*) or another participle (*The cat is on the a*). The sentence must read something like *The cat is on the roof.* Our intuitive knowledge of grammar allows us to make appropriate predictions, and the phonics of the last word of the sentence limits our choices (see chapter 6 on phonics). Similarly, our understanding of oral language allows us to read *the big gray cat* and not *the gray big cat*. If there is a grammatical reason, I don't remember it. It just doesn't sound right the other way, either when written or when spoken.

Learning the similarities and differences between written and oral language and intuiting the sounds of written language is initially achieved through hearing books read aloud.

Hearing books read aloud also exposes children to the sounds of literature. Nothing else provides this training. Children will bring this knowledge to the books they come to read.

Sitting close to the book-reading adult and looking at the book while it is being read aloud teaches children about the direction of print and how pages should be turned. It doesn't take long before a child will pick up a book independently and know precisely how to open it and turn the pages. Watching Mom or Dad read aloud also provides the child with many opportunities to see print. While seeing print—sometimes with the words being pointed out as they are read—the child begins to understand exactly what a written word is.

Talking with your child, encouraging oral language, provides him or her with a vocabulary that is useful and necessary for reading. Few young children will worry about words like *monotheistic*, but much language is learned in an environment enriched with experiences and discussion.

This is not to suggest that you put vocabulary words on flash cards or attempt to increase your child's vocabulary by five new words each week. It is a reassurance that an environment that includes reading aloud, experiences, and talk is the most critical "homework" that parents can do with children just emerging into literacy—and with children who are already literate. Do not minimize your role.

FIVE
Prediction and Literary Styles

The previous chapter discussed the importance of hearing written language so often that the language patterns become familiar. But not all written language patterns have the same style. Here are some examples of differing language styles:

Romeo, Romeo, Wherefore art thou, Romeo?
(Shakespeare)

It was the best of times, it was the worst of times . . .
(Dickens)

The government's chief auditor said Wednesday that taxpayers will have to spend $4 billion to bail out . . .
(newspaper)

Sergeant Johnson sat at his desk pondering the case.
(contemporary fiction)

Toast the pine nuts in the oven for fifteen minutes at 350 degrees.
(recipe)

Pesto-Stuffed Chicken Breasts . . . Skinned and boned chicken breasts stuffed with a spinach-ricotta filling and seasoned with pesto.
(menu)

The fog comes on little cat feet. It sits looking over harbor and city on silent haunches and then moves on.
("Fog," by Carl Sandburg)

Our ability to read and understand any of the above examples is determined by prior familiarity with each unique language pattern. Different types of literature have specific "ingredients" in much the same way as recipes do. Mysteries, for example, have different ingredients than those of romance novels. Ingredients include the combination of plot, mood, character type, setting, dialogue, and events that you come to expect whenever you read a book of a particular genre.

Stephen King fans have certain expectations of his horror novels because they know the kind of writer he is and the type of book he writes. Even before opening a Stephen King novel, the reader puts himself or herself in a certain state of mind, a different state of mind than when preparing to read a psychology textbook. This is no different than the way in which we prepare to watch a situation comedy on television as opposed to a PBS special on the fate of the African elephant. Once we are prepared for a particular type of literature, it is easy for us to make predictions when reading. This preparatory state of mind is critical to meaningful reading. Predictions become much easier to make.

There are many different types of children's books: folk tales, myths, tall tales, legends, to name just a few. All have qualities that make them unique.

Fairy tales, for example, have very specific elements that children should be familiar with. They begin with "Once upon a time" and end with ". . . and they lived happily ever after." Without a beginning and ending similar to this, it is not a fairy tale. Most fairy tales include magic, a beautiful young girl, royalty (perhaps a handsome young prince, an evil queen, or a rather nondescript king), an evil stepmother, an ugly witch, a clearly stated problem, and people and events that often occur in threes or sevens—or permutations and combinations of these elements.

These components become evident when children hear fairy tales read aloud many times. Children come to expect these elements before hearing (or reading) a new fairy tale. This preparatory state of mind is important to the reading process. If a child knows a fairy tale is to be read, it is not necessary to look at the first four words of the story to know its beginning. And if it doesn't begin precisely with the words "Once upon a time," then it will begin with something of similar meaning. Less specific, and just as important as the exact words, is the state of expectation a child has of the events that must occur for the story to be a fairy tale. A child doesn't consciously think, "Oh, I'm reading a fairy tale so there will be magic and a princess and a problem stated in the story." These are unspoken but well-understood expectations, which result from knowing about this type of literature. A child reading *Rapunzel* comes to a sentence about a "handsome young prince." Perhaps he or she does not recognize the word "prince," but knowing that it is a fairy tale eliminates the number of choices available and narrows it down to a particular character type.

The same is true for folk tales, myths, legends, and any other genres of literature. Even contemporary writers have specific styles where children learn to have expectations of the language and events of the stories. Judy Blume's *Tales of a Fourth Grade Nothing* or *Superfudge* are very different in sound and events than Roald Dahl's *Charlie and the Chocolate Factory* or *The BFG,* which in turn, are quite different from Paula Danziger's language and subject matter in *Remember Me to Harold Square* or *The Divorce Express*.

All literature has specific conventions and unique styles that, once understood through repeated readings, allow children to differentiate them. Once these different literary styles are expected, children make predictions as they read.

Having expectations does not mean we can predict exactly what will happen. The element of surprise is never lost. Learning the conventions of particular literary styles is like traveling around the English-speaking world and recognizing that although people of a different country share a common vocabulary and grammar, they often have very different language and cultural styles. Initial communication is sometimes difficult, but time spent listening to the language being spoken in that country and experiencing the culture simplifies the communication process. Once the "convention of the culture" is understood, communication is easier.

Making literature predictable to children is an identical process. Hearing all types of literature read aloud teaches children the conventions of those genres. The unique factors of each kind of literature—its language, character types, plot, dialogue, mood, and setting—is learned so that at some future independent reading, the literature will be easily predictable.

Knowing a particular genre of literature reduces the amount of visual information required to read. The predictions may not be exact, but the child has enough feeling for what is to occur (or to be said) that the predictions make sense.

I wish Shakespeare had been read to me long before my ninth-grade English class. *A Midsummer Night's Dream* might not have sounded as stilted, awkward, and completely incomprehensible as it did when I had to read my part orally to the class. Had I heard Dickens read aloud several years prior to opening up *Great Expectations*, I would not have relied completely on Cliff's Notes. It is unreasonable to expect anybody to read a piece of literature with fluency and comprehension merely because it is written in the English language.

All fluent readers, both young and old, consciously or unconsciously, predict. Without prediction, true reading does not occur.

SIX
The Role of Phonics

There are those who will defend teaching "reading through phonics" as fervently as the most loyal American might defend democracy.

There are hundreds of phonics programs available. Parents in North America spend a lot of money on phonics workbooks, phonics toys, phonics games, phonics computer programs, and phonics videos, all "guaranteed" to prepare children for reading and improve their reading abilities. Traditionally, some form of phonics instruction has been part of most school curricula. Some staff meetings could have used the Secretary of State to negotiate disagreements on phonetic approaches to reading.

The issue of phonics is an emotional hotbed. Parents take sides. Educators debate. Children get stuck in the phonetic middle.

Some of you turned to this chapter first. This is a testimony to parental concern over the phonics issue. If you are one of those parents, I suggest turning back to the beginning and reading the previous chapters. They are important in understanding the place that phonics has in reading. These chapters explain two important concepts: (1) we read for meaning, and (2) we predict the content as we read.

This does not mean that children ignore print and the sounds the letters make. But we need to put phonics in its proper c-o-n-t-e-x-t. (Sound it out! Say it fast! *Context!*)

I want to present the issue of phonics from a different perspective.

Pretend you are a tourist in Beverly Hills, California. You know that Beverly Hills is the city of the rich and famous, and you are on the lookout for movie stars and the luxury that surrounds them. As you window-shop down Rodeo Drive, noticing well-dressed individuals walking in and out of various boutiques, you glance to the street, hoping to see some of those luxurious automobiles you've heard that people drive in Beverly Hills. Lining the street, you see a pattern of Mercedes Benzes, Jaguars, and Porsches. Although you can't see it clearly, you notice a silver automobile approaching. You see its unique and distinctive grill; its RR emblem causes you to squeal with delight. You conclude that it must be a Rolls Royce. As the car passes, you see the size and shape of the vehicle, confirming that it is indeed a brand new Rolls.

It did not take much effort on your part to identify the Rolls Royce. You would probably not have expected a 1970 Pinto. This is not to degrade a Pinto, but several factors eliminated it as a likely candidate. First, your rich-and-famous frame of mind led you to believe that you would see a Rolls Royce before a Pinto. Second, your prior experience told you that a Rolls has a unique grill and an emblem with an engraved RR. This was probably all the information you needed to decide that the approaching vehicle, though you could not see it completely, was a Rolls Royce. You may ultimately have looked at the length of the body, the upholstery, and one or two other details, just to be certain. But it would not have been necessary to look at every aspect of this car to reach your conclusion. In terms of identification, it would have been a waste of time.

We have all been in situations where, because of the context, we expect to see something. We glance at only a part of the object but recognize it nonetheless. Our expectation, based on the context, is a sensible one. The same is true for all our perceptions. (Conversation, for example, occurs much too quickly to pay attention to each detail. When we listen to someone speak, we focus on the meaning, not on the words and sounds. We anticipate the speaker's ideas. Even if we have failed to hear every word clearly, we can usually figure out what was said by making sense of the message meant to be heard.)

Believe it or not, this episode is analogous to reading and the role of phonics. When we read, there is a defined context for reading, and the role of phonics is similar to seeing the emblem on the Rolls Royce. One or two features (letters) help you to narrow your choices.

Consider the following sentence:

I live in a _____.

Even though there are no letters to indicate the missing noun, we have a sense of the missing word, though we cannot be sure. If asked, you might think of twenty or more possibilities ranging from *house* to *cave,* depending upon the context of the story. If this is a story about a family in the suburbs, this limits our focus and probably eliminates choices like *houseboat* and *castle.* If this is a story about a homeless person, choices like *park* and *shelter* become possibilities. The meaning of the text helps eliminate unlikely possibilities.

But we need to narrow the choices a bit further, and this is where phonics helps. If we are reading about someone living in the suburbs, and the sentence reads: *I live in a . . .* we now predict what the next word will be, and the initial consonant *h* confirms our predictions by limiting our choices. The word cannot be *apartment, condominium,* or anything that doesn't begin with the letter *h,* so it's probably *house.* It *is* possible to read the word *home,* but that prediction makes sense and does not interfere with reading.

If I told you we were baking a cake and showed you the sentence *Separate three* _____ , you know that the missing word must be *eggs.* Little else makes sense.

Phonics confirms our predictions when reading *Mix the ba* _____ *with an ele* _____ *mi* _____ *for three m* _____ .

Mix the batter with an electric mixer for three minutes was easily determined when you could project meaning onto the page. There was no need to sound each word out. A few letters were enough. But no amount of phonics is useful if, when reading a recipe, you come across the word *roux* without ever having heard the word or anticipated it.

Overemphasizing phonics is confusing and misleading for several reasons:

1. The English language is very complex. There are, for example, more than fifty ways of pronouncing the letter *a* depending on the letters before and after it. A child may learn the *oo* in *moon* and then try to read *blood.* What about *ph* in *phoney* or the *th* in *thistle?* How might children generalize these with *shepherd* or *haphazard* or *nuthouse* and *penthouse.* Sure, phonics makes sense to adults because we already know the

words after seeing them so often. But for beginning readers, it is very confusing.

If you teach a child the "rule" that the *e* at the end of the word makes the vowel preceding the consonant long (*rate* or *like*, for example) how do you explain the pronunciation of such common words as *done, move, come, gone, are, one*, and *have?* If a child learns "when two vowels go walking the first one does the talking," how do they reconcile *relieve, great, sour*, and *brief?*

2. An overemphasis on phonics, particularly a "phonics-first" approach, does not make sense. There is no meaningful context for children. Phonics emphasizes teaching the parts of language (letters and sounds) first, with the larger picture (words, sentences, stories) coming only later. The casual observer must also distinguish between a child's ability to *mimic* phonics and a child's ability *to make sense* of phonics. Mimicry is simple, sounds good, and requires little more than the brains of a chimp. Making sense of phonics is much more complex.

3. Children can easily lose the meaning and purpose of reading if they learn from a phonics-first emphasis. Children instructed to read phonetically can easily be led to believe that reading is merely the act of attending to and stating sounds. Ignored, then, are the *ideas* of the story. Who can possibly concentrate on what the story is about if they are kept busy sounding out words? Or trying to recall the "controlled R" rule (*far, leader*, and so on)? And saying sounds faster and faster does not guarantee understanding; it just means saying the sounds faster. That's like keeping your car in

neutral and stepping on the accelerator. The RPMs increase, but you won't go anywhere.

With all this said, let's examine two final issues: phonics as a method of reading instruction, and how parents use phonics when reading to their child. Let's begin with school and end with the major thrust of this book—you and your child.

There are still many preschool and kindergarten programs in North America that spend a large part of the day teaching phonics. This usually includes learning the "letter of the week" in some seemingly harmless ways. If a particular week is devoted to teaching the letter *S,* a classroom is inundated with *S* projects, including flannelboard stories with the letter assuming anthropomorphic features (Sam the snake, with *S* looking very much like a snake), cooking spaghetti, forming cookie dough into an *S* and eating it, rotating one's body to form an S, singing "Sweet, Silly Songs," tracing *S*s in jello—and a host of other clever and cute *S* activities. Some classrooms build entire themes around one letter. More formal activities may include writing a page of *S*s and identifying pictures and objects that either end or begin with *S* or include *S* in the word. Many teachers are not this creative and provide daily phonics drills reminiscent of boot camp. (Yes, even some preschool teachers.)

Some may interpret these statements as my call for the elimination of the teaching of phonics in school. Not so. I do not know a single educator who would not agree that children need to understand some phonics. The differences lie in how phonetic knowledge is acquired and its application in reading. I argue against the kind of systematic and overdependent phonics instruction that may lead to confused readers, not better readers. I argue against spending an abundance of valuable time drilling letters and sounds, when time is better spent allowing children to hear, see, and read books. I feel it is no great tragedy if a preschool or kindergarten child happily skips off to the next grade without "knowing the letters." (I confess that many teachers at these grade levels would strongly disagree. Certainly much testing and evaluation at the early grades is based on a child's out-of-context knowledge of phonics.)

Parents worry so much about phonics instruction that—unfortunately—a preschool is often determined to be "good" or "not good" by how well (and creatively) its teachers teach the sounds to prepare children for kindergarten. Parents worry that a child who leaves kindergarten without knowing his or her sounds (or unable to blend the sounds together) will become a remedial first-grader. Parents frequently blame their child's reading problems on the lack of phonics (not realizing that sometimes these problems are the result of too much phonics!).

None of these "abilities" (to know sounds and to be able to blend them together) create more proficient readers. Does it really make sense that a thirty-year-old who had phonics instruction would be a better reader than a thirty-year-old who did not?

Too often parents take away from wonderful read-aloud time striving to create four-year-olds with PhDs in phonics. Instead of spending countless hours every week "phonic-ing" with your child, use the same time to read aloud, allowing the child to see the print. This is what a good teacher does—he or she immerses each child in print, just as you immersed your child in oral language. The more a child sees print, the more phonetic awareness develops. But it develops naturally, within a meaningful context.

There is nothing wrong with pointing out letters to your child or telling your child what their sounds are. Children who notice print are curious about letters and will ask you about them. Don't be afraid to discuss sounds when children ask (it's the ideal time), but don't go out to the nearest toy or computer store to buy the latest game, set of flash cards, or musical gimmick that guarantees the mastery of phonics.

It's hard—for parents and even for some teachers—to believe that phonics is not the essence of reading. A phonics approach should work, many believe, since we read words, and words are made up of letters. So many people in this country grew up learning phonics, that those of you who are fluent readers—and credit your phonics background for this—probably don't realize that you learned to read *in spite of* the heavy phonics emphasis in your education. You were lucky. Not everyone is.

You were probably read to a lot while growing up and given lots of opportunity to read for yourself.

Phonics should not be eliminated, just put in perspective. It's like the old Brylcreem hair tonic commercial: A little dab'll do ya!

SEVEN
The Stages of Reading

There are children who emerge naturally into literacy. That is, they begin to read with no formal instruction. I teach one or two of these children in my classroom each year. They know how to read when they come to school. I've asked parents of these children how these apparent miracles occurred. All respond similarly: they don't know. Most did no "formal teaching." Some did not discover that their child was reading until he (or she) was reading fluently. One day it seemed as if their child was not reading at all, the next day he was reading *War and Peace* between pacifiers.

Teachers have traditionally looked at those children who begin reading naturally—either before they came to school or effortlessly when they first arrive—as the anomalies of education. These children were usually labeled "gifted," placed in rapid-learner classrooms, and ignored as models for reading theory. We assumed that there was something unique about their brains. They were born genetically coded to read as naturally as they learned to walk.

In a sense, we were right. These children *were* born to read because they had home environments that were rich with books and print. More and more, educators are looking at these "gifted" children as models for reading instruction. We do not analyze their DNA structures but rather the environmental structures that nurtured this ability.

The single most important factor influencing children's literacy is the amount of time they are read to. Factors such as vitamins, low-cholesterol foods, or a private school education do not seem to matter. (Note, by the way, that I refer to quantity. Quality reading time one day a week is not as useful as reading aloud regularly seven days a week—even for only a few minutes.)

During the reading-aloud time, children experience books and print through the various stages that ultimately lead to independent reading. These stages are not necessarily sequential and independent of each other. They often overlap, mix, work in reverse, or occur at the same time. Nevertheless, they are present in the histories of children who naturally become fluent readers. Let me tell you about Nina.

1. *Learning to love books.* Shortly after Nina was born, her parents began to read to her. Nina would sit in her mother's lap and listen to stories. Initially, she didn't understand what this was all about, but she did understand the love, warmth, and security of that time on her mother's lap. Eventually, Nina associated this loving relationship with books. This association between love of parent and love of books is critical. A special time to "lap read" results in positive feelings for books and their connection with the most significant people in the child's life—as in Nina's case.

A parent who places familiar books in the child's crib, a parent who lovingly "lap reads" to the child at bedtime, is doing more than an obligatory parental activity with little or no consequence to the child's education. On the contrary, a parent who allows a child to associate books with love is helping to create attitudes that can never be duplicated in school. Making this association with books is vital in the early years. The longer it is delayed, the more difficult it is to capture later on. A child's love for books is fostered with early loving experiences.

2. *Enjoying the meaning in books.* As Nina grew older, she discovered that books are meant to say something. Books have meaning. Perhaps Mom or Dad read *This Little Piggie,* and Nina liked her toes wiggled. Maybe she was fascinated by the caterpillar in Eric Carle's *The Very Hungry Caterpillar.* She might have identified with Spot (*Where's Spot?*) and his mother's search for her lost puppy. She probably enjoyed Tomie dePaola's art in *Strega Nona,* or she enjoyed repeating "Clap, clap, stomp, stomp, nod, nod, wiggle, wiggle, and boo, boo" from *The Little Old Lady Who Was Not Afraid of Anything.* Nina listened and responded to the meaning of the books. Some stories had a delightful rhythm (*Brown Bear, Brown Bear*) and she joined in. Some books touched on her unconscious fears, hopes, and fantasies (*Snow White and the Seven Dwarfs*). And some stories were just plain fun to hear, with exciting plots, interesting characters, and perhaps funny situations. Whatever her reasons, Nina responded to the stories' meanings.

3. *Learning how books work.* During the first two stages, Nina learned the physical steps of maneuvering a book. She learned about turning pages. She learned about a book's format—which is the front cover and which is the back. Adults frequently assume a child understands how books work. Certainly adults don't think twice about it. While we may have memories of learning to read, we don't tend to have memories of learning how books work. We usually don't even think of it as something that has to be learned. While this is not formally taught, children must know this in order to read.

4. *Discovering that print has meaning.* While Nina responded to the meanings of stories, she also began to discover that those squiggles and lines on the page had something to do with the story and art. This was the print. Nina discovered that the story didn't come from Mom or Dad's imagination but from the print on the page. This was when Nina began to unlock the mystery of print.

    Nina continued to notice print in many contexts. She saw print on cereal boxes and her doll case. She saw print all around her in the environment and noticed how people responded to that print. As her family drove along a road, the car stopped at the sign that said *Stop*. The family looked for Nina's favorite restaurant. "There it is," she said. "McDonalds!" They drove by Nina's favorite department store. "Can we stop at Toys "Я" Us?" she exclaimed. "No," said Mom and Dad. "We're going to the movies now." As the family approached the theater, Mom pointed out "Cinderella" on the marquee.

Nina's days were filled with discovering print in her environment. Nina quite naturally wondered and asked about the letters as she became increasingly observant of print in the environment and print in books. *She* initiated questions about letters, which were (and should have been) answered with no dramatic fanfare. (The first time a child asks what sound a letter makes should not be the signal to buy a $75.00 computer program to teach phonics—just tell him.)

5. *Memorizing books.* Nina was fortunate when she was a toddler. Her parents were very patient. At bedtime, Nina would ask to hear a story. "Of course," her mother would smile. "Which story do you want to hear?" Beneath Mom's smile was terror. "Please," her mother said silently. "If there is a god in Heaven, Nina won't ask to hear *The Gingerbread Man* one more time. Please, please not that!" Nina looked at her mother with those sweet little eyes and said, "I want to hear the *The Gingerbread Man.*" Her mother secretly screamed, "AGH!!!!" but said gently to her daughter, "But you've heard that story for the past seventeen nights. Wouldn't you like to hear something else?" "No," said Nina. "I want to hear *The Gingerbread Man*," and, walking over half a dozen books lying on the floor, pulled from her messy bookshelf a tattered copy of her favorite book. She knew precisely where it was. Her mother sighed and opened the book. She could barely stand it, but Nina loved it. Nina had heard the book so many times that she had it memorized. If her mother made one mistake in a word, tried to skip a page, or left something out in order to expedite this reading time, Nina knew and would not allow it to occur. Nina had

memorized the exact content, the sequence of the story, and even when to turn the pages. Her mother and father, clever parents, had been able to sneak in a few dozen or so other books that had also become Nina's favorites at one time or other. Nina had heard and memorized many books.

6. *Rehearsing books.* If you think back to when your child began to talk, you remember how imprecise, inaccurate, and awkward it was. With lots of listening, unconditional acceptance, and a tremendous amount of practice, your child's language became increasingly accurate. This proficiency occurred quite naturally and predictably.

Nina did the same with books. One evening she decided to "read" one of her favorite books, one that she had heard many times at bedtime. She lay down on the carpet, opened the book to where the story began, and began to "read" the story herself. She probably paid little, if any, attention to the print. The illustrations guided her. (If you had covered up the illustrations, she would not have been able to "read" the book. She would probably have screamed "Nooooo!" and knocked your hand away.) The book's story was in her head. The illustrations jogged her memory.

Her "reading" was as imprecise as was her beginning speech. She frequently substituted her own vocabulary for the author's. She may have ignored large sections of the story, or left out parts that she nagged her parents about whenever they left them out when reading to her. However, she retold the story with assuredness and drama. The more she continued to hear this story read aloud, the more precise her retelling became. Eventually, it was exact.

From memory, children will precisely recreate lengthy pages of a book heard many times—a task that, as an adult, I couldn't do if I tried. I cannot explain why children are able to do this. Perhaps their minds are less cluttered than adults. Perhaps some stories are so meaningful to children that their power helps preserve their memory. Whatever the reason, Nina—and all young children—can rehearse a book in the same way that they practiced oral language when learning to speak.

Was Nina reading? Nina was turning the pages at the correct moment, attending to the ideas, content, and meaning of the story, but she did not focus on the print. In the classic sense, no, she was not reading. But she was like a new automobile that needs nothing but a little fuel to make it run.

7. *Recognizing the words.* The more Nina rehearsed books, the more attention she paid to the print. She even began to point to some of the words. This was her way of gaining control of the print. But most important, she was discovering what a written word is. She was making a connection, a bridge between rehearsing the book and seeing the print.

As she saw words again and again, she naturally began to recognize many of them in other meaningful contexts (in the same way that becoming familiar with a real-life dog in one situation means you will probably recognize a dog in another). There is a vast difference between recognizing words in meaningful contexts and trying to learn them by using flash cards. Drilling sight words on flashcards is pointless since they have no relationship to a larger piece of text.

8. *Developing fluency.* Nina's fluency and confidence increased. She still preferred reading books that she had already heard or ones to which she brought some background knowledge of content and vocabulary. Nina carefully studied the illustrations first and then read the text, actively predicting, then confirming her predictions based on the meaning that had developed from her reading. Nina's recognition of letters aided in her predictions. Obviously, she paid attention to the print at a much more detailed level than ever before. She approximated the language of the book and was accurate enough to make sense.

9. *Independent reading.* Today Nina picks up either a familiar or an unfamiliar book and can read it independently and with understanding. She reads with a clear balance between prediction and focusing on the print. Sight, again, acts to confirm her predictions. Her reading may not be 100 percent accurate, but she self-corrects if her predictions don't make sense. She is very familiar with the phonics of words, but only pays attention to phonics as necessary. Nina has enough knowledge of sight words that, if asked, she could locate any word on the page. (Why she would have to do this ridiculous task is anybody's guess!) She is, by anyone's standards, a reader.

Increased fluency and independence involve a variation on all these stages of reading.

Older children need lap and bedtime reading too. Upper elementary children still need to hear meanings in books, meanings that can only come from hearing books read aloud. A fourth-grade child may not memorize *Charlie and the Chocolate Factory* verbatim, but will remember familiar portions of the book—characters, setting, conflicts, language style, and dialogue—when reading independently. A sixth-grade child will want to read *The Black Stallion* independently after hearing the book read aloud. We all like the familiar. That is one reason why books that have been made into films or television series sell so well after the public sees them. The stories are familiar, and familiarity is comfortable.

This is not to say that if you read to your children from birth that they will read before kindergarten. Children read when all forces say go. Some children take longer to begin reading than others. Children develop differently. It is impossible to rush children because it cannot be done. No one tries to hurry a woman's gestation period so that a child will be delivered in five months. No one tries to get a baby to walk in its first three months. Babies are born when it is time. Toddlers walk when they are ready. Children talk when they are ready. And children begin to read when they are ready.

The reason that walking and talking occurs without much worry is because we trust children. We trust that they'll learn to walk and we trust that they'll talk. We must also trust that they will read.

I realize that there are reading programs in which children, at an early age, learn to blend sounds or read sight words. This also occurs in many classrooms. Children learn to combine phonics and sight words to say sentences. This may impress some parents, relieve many teachers, and provide "advanced" test scores to administrators. But saying sounds and words, no matter how quickly and fluently, is not reading. Reciting a list of words, no matter how polysyllabic, provides nothing but a false sense of security and assurance about a child's reading.

EIGHT

Some Don'ts and Do's When Reading with Your Child

Parents often ask their child's teacher what they can do at home to reinforce their child's reading instruction. This is sometimes a polite way of asking for homework. Whenever parents asked this of me when I was first teaching, I always told them to read aloud to their children. This was not necessarily the kind of answer they wanted. Reading aloud just didn't seem substantive enough. But once they accepted this as the only homework I would assign (I have softened up a bit since then—in chapter 9 I talk about some other things that parents can do), parents asked if there was anything that they should be aware of to avoid "conflicting" with my teaching style. Initially I could not imagine how reading aloud (or, with beginning readers, listening to their child read aloud) could possibly interfere with reading instruction. But I soon discovered that some parents—usually those with the best intentions—can interfere not only with reading instruction but also with a child's emerging literacy. Unwittingly, some of the most loving parents have unrealistic expectations for their child's beginning reading. These can become translated into "assignments" and turn reading into a chore instead of a joy for their child.

Eventually, I sent home a letter to all parents explaining what not to do, either when reading aloud or when listening to their children read. Aside from several extra paragraphs about lunch money, upcoming field trips, and our winter break, this is the letter.

Dear Parents,

Many of you have asked for specific ways that we can work in tandem to help your child's reading. I know I have encouraged you to read *to* your child and listen to your child read to you. While I don't think you can ever make a mistake reading aloud to your child, there are some pitfalls you should try to avoid so that you do not spoil your child's enjoyment in learning to read. Here are some "don'ts" to keep in mind:

1. Don't insist that your child "sound out" unknown words. This is tedious, boring, and the results will seldom be accurate. Much of the English language is difficult to "sound out." Even if a child is successful, the meaning of the passage can be lost. Children can't possibly focus on meaning when they're expending their efforts focusing on sounds. Instead, encourage a child to guess what a word is or might be. What makes sense in the context of a sentence, a paragraph, or a story is much more important than total accuracy. There is nothing wrong with casually asking a child what a word in a sentence might be if it begins with, for example, *b*. But meaning must come before phonetics. Remember, too, that the size and configuration of a word help determine its meaning. "This looks like a long word," says the adult to the child. "What long word do you think it might be?"

2. Don't discourage finger pointing. Have you ever noticed that when adults read unfamiliar material, they will sometimes point to the words? Finger pointing helps us gain control over the text. Children point to words for the same reason. In fact, if it doesn't distract from the enjoyment of reading, you might consider pointing to the words as you read aloud, especially with simpler texts. In the ed biz this is called "tracking," and it is a useful strategy that is frequently used in classrooms. When children gain confidence in their reading, they give up finger pointing.

3. Don't teach your child rules for sounding out words. They are confusing, frustrating, and often inaccurate. They interfere with meaning and remove the joy from reading. How can anyone ever know what is happening in a story if constantly thinking of "if two vowels go walking, the first one does the talking"? How can a child enjoy a story worrying about whether the letter *c* has a "hard" or "soft" pronunciation? And these are only two rules. Suppose you had to remember a dozen rules for just one story!

4. Don't force your child to read (or listen to you read) if he or she doesn't want to. While you want to encourage and support that effort, children learn best when they have the power to do so themselves; they don't need to be forced, threatened, or bribed. Children learn to speak because communication is a tremendous and innate need. The need for communication through literacy—reading and writing—will also come to them. Forcing children to read only makes them angry and defiant. If my child refused to read (or to listen to me read aloud) I would ask myself why: Is

she frustrated? Does she feel I'm going to criticize her? Is the reading material boring or irrelevant? Doesn't she find the illustrations attractive and interesting? Are there different kinds of books, such as flip-up books, that my child would enjoy? Don't hesitate to ask your child about his or her interests. Very often he (or she) will be able to tell you.

5. Don't teach your child words by drilling him or her with flashcards. This is of little value to your child's reading. Just because a child can recite 220 frequently used words does not mean that he or she will be able to read them in a sentence or story. When they first begin reading, children will recognize words within meaningful context but seldom out of context. Children learn to recognize isolated words only after they have practiced reading them within context many, many times.

6. Don't correct every reading error your child makes. If you do, do not be surprised if your child becomes hesitant and unenthusiastic about reading, anxious about making errors, and discouraged about him- or herself. Many children who receive this "immediate feedback" never want to read. Why should they? No one wants somebody pouncing on every error they make. Besides, errors that children make are often "sensible" errors. That is, they make sense within the context of the story and don't change the meaning of the story at all. And nagging children about every error can only prevent them from correcting their own mistakes. They will know it's a mistake if it doesn't make sense then or as they read further.

Children learn by making errors in environments—school and home—that not only accept mistakes but positively encourage them. Think back to when your child learned to speak. Your child made a garbled attempt at the word "Mommy." The pronunciation wasn't even close. You phoned grandparents, aunts, uncles, and other relatives to show off. And you probably praised your child's mispronunciation of hundreds of other words. No one worried that complimenting the child's mistakes would cause incorrect speech. The more your child heard and practiced the language, the more precise your child's language became.

For the first years of children's lives, we reinforce many mistakes to create an environment in which they feel free to risk. We must maintain that same "freedom to risk" once children enter school. Otherwise, children will only do what they feel can be accomplished successfully. How would you feel if your supervisor (or spouse) criticized every error you made?

7. Don't worry about the number of times you read the same book to your child. Children love hearing the same books read a million times, and they love reading those books just as often. They'll read the same book over and over until the meaning is exhausted. This should be encouraged, not discouraged. As children become familiar with a book, they will repeat it with the reader. At first their eyes will wander around the page, probably focusing on the illustrations. Eventually they will try to follow the print. If it doesn't interfere with the enjoyment, here is your opportunity to point to the words. This will help your children learn

about print. As your children hear the same book again and again, they prepare for the anticipated parts and begin to look ahead for the words—before they are read. This is no different than learning any other activity initiated by an adult. Slowly but surely children develop some independence and ultimately take over the activity unassisted.

8. Last, but far from least, don't expect your child to actively engage in reading if he or she never sees you read. We serve as models for children. They pick up our good points and our bad points. This is as true for a teacher as it is for a parent. (My most agonizing yet insightful moments have been watching children in my classroom playing teacher.) If children do not have adult role models who read, they see little purpose behind reading. Make certain that you read and that your child sees you reading. This is just as important as reading *to* your child. Lecturing and discussing the importance of reading is unimportant and unproductive. Silently modeling reading says it all. This is not "fake" reading for effect; it is real reading for a sustained period of time. I don't care if you read a book, newspaper, magazine, or trashy novel. You must be an honest model for your child in all areas, including reading.

Sincerely,

Steve

Steve

This was my letter. Parents from year to year said that it was helpful. I hope that you agree.

NINE

When Reading Aloud
Is Not Enough—
A Short Play

SCENE: A kindergarten or grade-one classroom

TIME: Tonight, about 9:00 P.M.

SITUATION: It is back-to-school night. Thirty-five parents have just listened to the teacher explain this year's reading philosophy, a brilliant summation, reflecting the philosophy of the book *Raising Readers*. (He has also suggested that each parent get a copy.)

CHARACTERS:

The parents. A group of sophisticated and concerned parents who have a reputation among the staff for requesting additional activities to do with their children at home to encourage reading.

The teacher. A dedicated, hard-working individual who cannot understand why parents feel that they must do something more than just read aloud to their child.

Teacher: Are there any more questions?

Parent 1 (who has been scratching her head and looking confused during most of the presentation): So, I'm still not clear. There's nothing more I can do with my child at home?

Parent 2: My older son had Mrs. Kimball in kindergarten, and she gave him twenty nursery rhymes to memorize.

Parent 3: And my neighbor's son goes to The Day School, and they send home a three-page letter of things to do with your child to help improve reading.

Teacher (resisting): I know it's popular to provide activities, I just don't think that they are particularly useful.

Parent 1: We want homework! We want homework! *(Several parents join in. They stand up holding protest signs and march around the room chanting, "What do we want? Homework! When do we want it? Now!")*

Teacher: Okay, okay. Put your signs away and sit down. I'll tell you some other things that you can do with your child. I just want to caution you: Don't use these activities to replace valuable reading time with them. And if your child is bored or unresponsive to these activities, don't try to lure him or her with rewards or threaten with punishment to get him or her to participate.

Parent 2: We promise.

Teacher: First of all, do any of you read in front of your child?

Parent 1: I usually read in bed.

Parent 2: And fall asleep after five minutes.

Teacher: I think that's true for many of us. But it's important for your child to see you as a reader. I suggest scheduling a reading time with your child. Maybe not every day, but choose five days a week where, for at least ten minutes, each member of the family will read in the presence of each other.

Parent 3: Read a book?

Teacher: Newspapers and magazines are fine. But everyone should read. Your child should have something to read too.

Parent 1: This is in addition to reading aloud to my child?

Teacher: Yes.

Parent 2: I just know that my child will come over, sit on my lap, and pretend to read what I'm reading.

Teacher: That's fine. This is not so much a rehearsal time for your child as it is a modeling time.

Parent 1: Gosh, I hate reading.

Teacher: Then don't be surprised if your child hates reading too. The most important lessons children learn about literacy are from your actions, not your words.

Parent 4: I think that my child should have flashcards to learn sight words.

Teacher (beginning to buckle under the pressure): I've got an idea. I'll suggest a flashcard activity, but a meaningful one. Give your child a blank sheet of paper to draw a picture. Ask him to tell you something about the picture in one or two sentences. Print your child's description *exactly as your child has stated it.* Don't change the words or correct the grammar! Print those words directly on the page as well as on a strip of paper about two inches by eight inches. Cut the strip into individual words. Now the activity becomes a game of placing the words in the correct order.

Parent 1: Can they use the sentence you've written on the page to help?

Teacher: That's why it's there. If it helps, they can place the word cards underneath the sentence. A more sophisticated activity would be without the use of the sentence.

Parent 4: Should they read the words like flashcards?

Teacher (beginning to sweat): No, but after your child has had lots of experience putting the words in the correct order, mix the cards up and practice them out of order. But if it makes your child anxious, stop.

Parent 2: How many sentences and how many days a week?

Teacher: No more than two sentences during one sitting and probably only once or twice a week.

Parent 4: Should I drill the words?

Teacher: Again, try to keep the words within the context of a sentence rather than in meaningless isolation.

Parent 3: Hmph! Seems like Mickey Mouse education to me.

Teacher: After a while, you'll have a collection of words. I'd suggest putting these in a big envelope or a file folder. With a collection of words you can make up silly sentences that your child can change to make sense. For example, using your child's words, you might create: "I live in a dog." Your child can find a word that makes better sense. Notice that I began the sentence sensibly. That's important to establish some meaning. Your child will also have fun making up silly sentences.

Parent 1: We've done this since my little Davey was seven months old, and he's doing quite well. He now recognizes more than 500 words and can factor pi. But he's tired of drawing pictures and just wants to tell us the words.

Teacher: That's fine. The picture drawing helps some kids think of the sentence.

Parent 4: I *love* that. What other flashcard ideas do you have?

Teacher: Children are familiar with food cartons—cereal boxes, milk containers. After you've finished with the cartons, cut out these familiar words and add them to their collection.

Parent 1: Will my child then be able to read these words in books?

Teacher: "Jello," "Lucky Charms," and "Crest" don't usually appear in books but do occur in everyday use.

Parent 2: Are there other things to do?

Teacher: You could try labeling things around the house, perhaps starting in your child's room with things that are meaningful to a child, things like "toy box."

Parent 2: Just write "toy box"?

Teacher: Why not write an entire sentence or phrase such as "This is Mike's toy box" or "Jason's dresser." You could also ask your children what they would like labeled and what they would like the labels to say.

Parent 4 (excitement building): And then put those words on flashcards!

Teacher: Another suggestion is to write notes to your child. Your handwriting should be large and clear. A simple note in their lunchbox saying "I love you," or "I hope you're having a nice day," not only encourages reading, but conveys other important messages that mean a lot to a child.

Parent 1: They can't read those words.

Teacher: Someone in the cafeteria will read them for your child. But don't feel the need to write something different each day. Repetition of certain notes will help a child read them independently one day.

Parent 4: Is there anything else that parents can do?

Teacher: Pointing out signs as you drive is always useful. Children love environmental print. When you notice your bank, you can say, "See that sign? Your entire college education was lost in that failed savings and loan." This not only points out the name of the bank, but also the state of our dwindling economy!

Parent 3: Is there something that we can do while we read together?

Teacher: Sure. As you're reading aloud, stop before stating the next word and ask your child to guess what it will be. After your child guesses, read the rest of the sentence to see if it makes sense.

Dramatizing stories is always fun too. "Pat-a-cake, pat-a-cake" is a perfect example of a nursery rhyme that allows for easy, relaxed pretending. It's fun to "bake a cake" together and then "put it in the oven for baby and me." Dramatization helps bring meaning to the story. Extend this idea and really bake a cake together. As you do, occasionally recite the rhyme. Literature should, as often as possible, connect to the real world. That's why, if you read something about a farm for example (and don't live on one), you should try to find a farm to visit if you can.

Parent 1: Pat a cake are three of the 500 words my son knows by sight. You won't have to teach him those.

Teacher: Thank you. That's a relief!

Parent 2: What about asking questions to make sure that my child understands the story?

Teacher: I have no doubt that your child will understand the story without your questions, but discussing the story with your child is still valuable. Focus on discussions that go beyond superficial notions that textbooks emphasize like "the main idea" or "the main character." We want children to think critically. Talk about the funniest part of the story or the silliest thing that happened to one of the characters. Ask if the story ended the way they expected. How might they change the ending? Ask what ideas the story made them think about. Ask if the story made them feel a certain way, and tell them if any part of the story caused you (the parent) to feel reflective, happy, or sad. Literature touches us emotionally, and it's useful for children to reflect upon that. Think about the kinds of family discussions you've had after you've watched a movie or television show together. Above all—*don't overdo it.* Emphasizing questions, especially for a young child, can be a hindrance.

Parent 3: I asked my child to point to a word on the page and he pointed to the letter.

Teacher: It's hard to know exactly what that means. Some children believe letters are words, but they begin to understand about words if you point to them as you read aloud. There are, however, other terms we assume children understand, but they may not: A book's "title" and "author" are just two that you might want to mention.

Parent 1: I think I'm on idea overload!

Teacher: But I'm on a roll. There is an inextricable . . .

Parent 4: Is *inextricable* one of their sight words?

Teacher: Next year. There is an inextricable link between reading and writing. Even though it may seem like scribbling to you, children's pretend writing is important in many respects. Writing is another way that children begin to understand how print works—both the sounds and the words.

If your child has plenty of blank paper, pencils, pens, and markers, and is surrounded with a literate environment—books, magazines, newspapers, labels, posters on their walls, and parents who are seen reading and writing—it is hard to imagine a child not wanting to write. Kids will ask you to help them, and you must be patient and provide the information they ask for. They will ask you how to make a *p* and you must show them. When they write a letter to Grandma, they will ask, "How do you spell 'dear'?" and you must tell them. Eventually, after some confidence has been established, encourage them to guess what the spelling might be, and compliment them on their guess (even if it isn't correct). Don't worry about correcting them. Try to create real reasons for children to write. Thank-you notes are always good. Some children are pen pals of relatives or friends who live out of town.

And as with reading, children need to see parents as models for writing. Write your own letters in front of your child. Share your letters with him or her. Have your child add one thought to your letter, even if it's a scribble. At the least, your child can sign his or her name.

Parent 3: Do you have any suggestions for places to keep all the things you think our kids should have? I mean, writing and drawing materials, books, magazines—their rooms will look like junkyards.

Teacher: You're right; they'll be cluttered. But your goal is exactly that. Surround them with literacy in the same way that they were initially surrounded by talk. Children who come from homes with few, or inaccessible, books have fewer opportunities to interact with those books. Anyway, I suspect that you can come up with ways to manage the mess. If you expect a four- or five-year-old to maintain an impeccably tidy environment, and you do so by prohibiting relatively free access to materials, you will have to accept the consequences of those actions. That may mean a child for whom books will always have little importance.

Parent 1: Thank you. I think I've had enough.

Parent 2: Yes, you've convinced me. It's midnight now, and I should probably be getting home.

Parent 3: We'll try your suggestions. They sounded great.

Parent 4: Now, one more time. Did you say I could buy those sight-word flashcards at the local teacher's store?

(The parents slowly leave, taking several of the leftover cookies for the drive home. The teacher turns out the one light in the classroom that works, shuts the door, and in the middle of the darkness, emits a blood-curdling scream.)

(Lights fade.)

TEN

Rhyme, Rhythm, and Repetition— Predictable Literature

A sign on the wall of my health club reads "No pain, no gain." The implication was that the road to a goal must be difficult and frustrating; otherwise the goal isn't rewarding, beneficial, or attainable. The "No pain, no gain" sign has now been removed. Some intuitive soul realized that if exercise hurts, it's harmful.

"No pain, no gain" is no more true in the classroom than in the gym. The child who struggles when learning to read does not enjoy reading, does not become a fluent reader, and will often develop reading difficulties.

Learning to read should be made as easy as possible. Children should learn to read naturally and joyfully, no differently than the Ninas of the world. Nina, who you met in chapter 7, heard books, memorized books, and rehearsed books—all in a loving, supportive environment. To assist children with this "effortless" task of learning how to read, we can provide them with a type of book that allows for easy memorization. These are predictable books.

I've written about the importance of prediction in reading and how experiences and knowledge of how literature sounds aid in these predictions. But literature can also be purposefully written to be predictable, enabling beginning readers to enter the world of literacy with no pain and lots of gain.

Authors of predictable books know that children love the 3Rs: rhyme, rhythm, and repetition. They know that children naturally try to predict what the next word, words, or sentence in a story will be. They know that children enjoy repetition in a story. They know that children love rhythmic chanting and do it almost instinctively when they play. (Remember jump-rope chants?) They know that all children like to feel immediately successful when reading, so these writers write stories that are interesting, well-written, and have fun with language.

I've classified predictable books into nine categories: picture-matching books, substitution books, cumulative books, response books, books with repeated portions, interlocking books, rhythmic books, poetry, and songs to read. Some books cannot be classified into a single category, because they fit into more than one.

1. *Picture-matching books.* These books have texts that correspond precisely with the pictures. The text on each page may be one or two words, a phrase, or a sentence. Rarely are there more than a few sentences in a picture-matching book. In *Rosie's Walk,* Pat Hutchins tells the story of Rosie the hen's walk through the farm, calmly avoiding capture by a fox. Each preposition corresponds to an illustration as Rosie walks:

across the yard
around the pond
over the haystack
past the mill
through the fence
under the beehives
and back home in time for dinner

Many other books present text in the same manner. Robert Kalan's *Rain* (with illustrations by Donald Crews) is another fine example:

TEXT	ILLUSTRATION
Blue sky	picture of a blue sky
Yellow sun	picture of a yellow sun
White clouds	picture of white clouds

The text continues in a similar pattern showing the development of a rainstorm. Then it continues by naming other colorful places that the rain falls, ending with a rainbow. (All of Donald Crews's raindrops are marvelously illustrated with tiny letters that spell "rain.")

2. *Books with substitutions.* These books are similar to picture-matching books in that they match pictures to text. However, sentences remain almost identical on each page except for the substitution of a word. Each time a new animal sits on a mat in Brian Wildsmith's *Cat on the Mat* there is less and less room for the cat.

The cat sat on the mat.
The dog sat on the mat.
The goat sat on the mat.
The cow sat on the mat.
The elephant sat on the mat.
(*The cat hisses them all away and is now happily left alone.*)
The cat sat on the mat.

Books with substitutions change several words or a short phrase, still maintaining the basic sentence structure, as in bp nichol's *Once: A Lullaby* (illustrated by Anita Lobel):

Once I was a little horse,
baby horse, little horse.
Once I was a little horse.
NEIGH, I fell asleep.

Once I was a little cow,
baby cow, little cow.
Once I was a little cow.
MOO, I fell asleep.

The same pattern follows throughout the book, with a different animal and animal sound substituted on each page.

3. *Books that are cumulative.* These books start with one sentence, adding another sentence with each successive page, always repeating the previous sentences. The most famous version of this type of book is *The House That Jack Built:*

This is the house that Jack built.

This is the malt
That lay in the house that Jack built.

This is the rat
That ate the malt
That lay in the house that Jack built.
This is the cat,
That killed the rat
That ate the malt
That lay in the house that Jack built.

This nursery rhyme has been retold with delightful variations as in Joan Heilbroner's *This Is the House Where Jack Lives:*

This is the house where Jack lives.
This is the dog that lives in the house where Jack lives.
This is the boy that walked the dog that lives in the house where Jack lives.
This is the pail that fell on the boy . . .

Audrey and Don Woods' *The Napping House* provides a further example of a cumulative text:

There is a house,
a napping house,
where everyone is sleeping.
And in that house
there is a bed,
a cozy bed
in a napping house,
where everyone is sleeping.
And on that bed
there is a granny,
a snoring granny
on a cozy bed
in a napping house,
where everyone is sleeping.

4. *Response books.* These often come in the form of questions and answers. Robert Kraus's *Whose Mouse Are You?* (with illustrations by José Aruego), a modern day classic, follows this format:

Whose mouse are you?
Nobody's mouse.
Where is your mother?
Inside the cat.

Where is your father?
Caught in a trap.
Where is your sister?
Far from home.

Whose Mouse Are You? is easily memorized, contains illustrations that correspond with the text, and has a happy ending after relating a sad tale of loss.

Mirra Ginsburg's *Where Does the Sun Go at Night?* follows a similar format:

Where does the sun go at night?
To his grandma's house.
Where does he sleep?
In his grandma's bed.
Who is his grandma?
The deep blue sky.
What is he covered with?
A woolly cloud.

Mirra Ginsburg's *The Chick and the Duckling* is a response book that is not in the usual question-answer format:

A duckling hatched out of its shell.
"I am out," said the duckling.
"Me too," said the chick.
"I am going for a walk," said the duckling.
"Me too," said the chick.
"I am walking," said the duckling.
"Me too," said the chick.

This book contains a dramatic climax that is resolved in a comfortable and humorous way.

5. *Repeated portions within books.* These books usually have one to four lines that repeat throughout the tale. The traditional examples of these books are fairy tales

and folk tales. In *Snow White* the wicked queen/witch time and time again asks her mirror:

> Mirror, mirror on the wall,
> Who's the fairest one of all?

Children will join in each and every time this is read. The same is true for the folk tale *The Three Little Pigs*. Three times the wolf and pig have a most frightening encounter:

> "Open up and let me in!"
> "Not by the hair of my chinny-chin-chin."
> "Then I'll huff and I'll puff and I'll blow your house in!"

The Little Red Hen contains this lazy refrain four or five times, depending on the version:

> "Not I!" said the dog.
> "Not I!" said the cat.
> "Not I!" said the mouse.
> "Then I will," said the little red hen.
> And she did.

All of these classic tales have been retold by contemporary authors. Most notable is author Paul Galdone. He has taken great pains to maintain the integrity of each tale, provided the repetition of language, and added his exciting illustrations. There are, however, numerous contemporary books offering the same repetition. In George Shannon's *Lizard's Song*, Lizard sings his song throughout the book:

> Zoli, zoli, zoli—zoli, zoli, zoli,
> Rock is my home—rock is my home
> Zoli, zoli, zoli—zoli, zoli, zoli

Another book by the same author, *Dance Away,* has Rabbit dancing and singing his dancing song eleven times:

Left, two, three, kick
Right, two, three, kick
Left skip, right skip
Turn around

Mem Fox's *Hattie and the Fox* is the story of five barnyard animals who see a fox slowly emerge from the bushes. Every time another part of the fox's body is revealed, there is a rousing refrain of indifference:

"Good grief!" said the goose.
"Well, well!" said the pig.
"Who cares?" said the sheep.
"So what?" said the horse.
"What next?" said the cow.

6. *Rhythmic books.* These books are so full of rhythm that they are great fun to read aloud. They are like music without the melody. Rhythmic books often have a rhyming pattern as well. Bruce Degan's *Jamberry* is not rock'n'roll, it's rollick'n'roll. *Jamberry* is loved by both children and adults:

One berry
Two berry
Pick me a blueberry.
Hatberry
Shoeberry,
In my canoeberry.
Under the bridge
And over the dam,
Looking for berries,
Berries for jam.

Almost every kindergarten classroom in North America has at least one copy of Bill Martin Jr.'s *Brown Bear, Brown Bear, What Do You See?* Once you and your child read it together, you will see why this book has remained popular for over twenty years. I initially placed this book under the category of "picture-matching books," but its rhythm won out. The first page restates the title, with a picture of a brown bear. When you turn the page, the book continues:

> I see a red bird looking at me.
> Red bird, red bird, what do you see?

On this page there is a picture of a red bird. The text continues on the following page:

> I see a yellow duck looking at me.
> Yellow duck, yellow duck, what do you see?

The book continues like this for fifteen pages, each illustrated with an animal of a different color. The rhythm of the chant makes the book fun to repeat aloud. The illustration on each page corresponds exactly with the text on that page.

7. *Interlocking books.* Interlocking books are like a circle of toppling dominoes. As each domino falls it pushes the next one over until the last domino touches the first. Confused? Keiko Kosza's *When the Elephant Walks* will clarify what I mean:

> When the elephant walks . . .
> he scares the Bear.
> When the Bear runs away . . .
> he scares the Crocodile.
> When the Crocodile swims for his life . . .

he scares the Wild Hog.
When the Wild Hog dashes for safety . . .
he scares Mrs. Raccoon.
When Mrs. Raccoon flees with her baby . . .
they scare the little Mouse.
But when the little Mouse scurries in terror . . .
. . . Well, who would be scared by a little Mouse?

There is a final illustration of an elephant. The story
has come full circle. Not all interlocking stories come
full circle in the same way, but they share a similar
structure, as in Remy Charlip's *Fortunately:*

Fortunately one day Ned got a letter that said, "Please
come to a Surprise Party."
But unfortunately the party was in Florida and he
was in New York.
Fortunately a friend loaned him an airplane.
Unfortunately the motor exploded.
Fortunately there was a parachute in the airplane.
Unfortunately there was a hole in the parachute.

Through both fortunate and unfortunate circumstances,
Ned eventually arrives at the surprise party.

8. *Books of poetry.* As previously mentioned, children
should be given the opportunity to hear a variety of
poetic styles read aloud. Poems by such poets as David
McCord, Leland B. Jacobs, Jack Prelutsky, Eve
Merriam, Karla Kuskin, and N. M. Bodecker are
found in anthologies of children's poetry or collections of each poet's own works. Some of these individual poems may ultimately find their way into book
form, but as this chapter emphasizes predictable books
that help immerse children in print, I will refer only to
single poems in book form.

Tomie dePaola illustrated Sarah Hale's poem, *Mary Had a Little Lamb*. As Tomie explains in his foreword to that book, this version includes the poem's "exact wording, original spacing, gender, and punctuation from 1830 . . . ." The book works like a picture-matching book with the text matching the illustrations. *Humpty Dumpty* also works like a picture-matching book. Stephen Weatherill's illustrations have the added attraction of occasionally fitting together like a puzzle. Fun with illustrations can also be said for Colin and Jacqui Hawkins's book *Old Mother Hubbard*. It is a lift-the-flap book. After you read: "Old Mother Hubbard went to the cupboard to get her poor dog a bone," the child lifts the flap of the cupboard, and notices an empty shelf with the words, "But when she got there the cupboard was bare /So the poor dog gave a groan." Innovation is also the hallmark of Ian Beck's *Little Miss Muffet,* with this version performed on stage with eight different scenes. The book begins with the traditional tale but quickly moves on to variations:

> Little Miss Muffet sat on a tuffet,
> eating her curds and whey,
> When along came the Sun, bringing hours of fun,
> You'll need me to brighten your play.
>
> Then along came . . .
> a brush, a broom, and a mop,
> all cleaning away, they just couldn't stop.
> We'll sweep you up too, if you stay!
>
> Then along came four mice, you weren't very nice,
> We're Sneaky, and Slinky, and Shifty, and Stinky
> and we'll steal all your goodies away.

Even Robert Frost's *Stopping by Woods on a Snowy Evening* will appeal to young readers, thanks to Susan Jeffers's illustrations:

> Whose woods these are I think I know.
> His house is in the village, though;
> He will not see me stopping here
> To watch his woods fill up with snow.

Hopefully, more and more delightful poetry will find its way to book form.

9. *Books to sing.* Many popular children's songs have been "novelized." Children often know the song long before they see the book, so can "read" the book comfortably. The favorite Thanksgiving song, *Over the River and Thro' the Woods* has recently been illustrated by Normand Chartier. Aliki's version of *Go Tell Aunt Rhody* tells the tragic story of that old and dead grey goose. There are several excellent versions of *Ten in the Bed*. Tracey Campbell Pearson has humorously illustrated both verses of *Sing a Song of Sixpence*. Illustrator Paul Galdone's *Over in the Meadow* and *Three Blind Mice* are delights to the eye and ear. Children's recording artist, Raffi, has published many of his popular songs in this format. Two of these are *Shake My Sillies Out* and *Down by the Bay*. Some familiar songs have been reborn with new lyrics. Elizabeth Lee O'Donnell has given *The Twelve Days of Christmas* new life in her version entitled *The Twelve Days of Summer:*

> On the first day of summer,
> I sat down by the sea
> A little purple sea anemone.

On the second day of summer,
I sat down by the sea
Two pelicans
And a little purple sea anemone.

On the third day of summer,
I sat down by the sea
Three jellyfish,
Two pelicans,
And a little purple sea anemone.

One final reminder about predictable books: While they allow for easy memorization and independent rehearsal, a child's library should not be restricted to only this kind of book. There are many wonderful read-alouds that belong in a child's library that do not fit into the previous categories. The following chapter offers you some further guidelines to help you choose all kinds of books that children will want to read.

ELEVEN
Choosing a Good Children's Book

Talk about setting myself up for criticism! I might be safer with a chapter entitled "Choosing a Good Mate" or "How to Choose a Good Religion." The operationally explosive word here is "good," and its use is judgmental and subjective. I do not write this chapter from a literary critic's perspective but as an adult who works a lot with kids and believes that they deserve to eat the best food, have the best parents, play with the best friends, and enjoy the best toys. They also deserve to hear and read the best books.

Clearly children don't always play with "educational toys" or have the friends we wish for them, and most of them love eating junk food. I love Twinkies too, but a daily diet is probably not recommended. Children may love the latest book based on a cartoon character or toy, but that doesn't mean a steady diet of that kind of book is recommended either. Children enjoy many things that parents can't and shouldn't provide—television for ten hours a day, ice cream on demand, computer games instead of bed.

Many books that children bring to school are the literary version of Twinkies. Children may enjoy them, want to hear them again and again, and love "reading" them, but they are "junk food" nevertheless. It has always distressed me when a five-year-old bounces into my classroom at 8:00 A.M. with a book that his or her mother or father bought the previous night at the grocery store, which instantly became this child's favorite. You know the one. You can find it on the rack of the grocery store (or toy store), usually near the checkout stand. It sells for about $3.95. After skimming through, it's easy to see how little thought was put into the publication. It may have been modeled after a popular Saturday morning cartoon. If this isn't bad enough, the book has fifty pages with lots of words on each page, and the child expects me to read it to the entire class. It will take forever. With my kindest voice and a smile on my face, I tell the child "I'll read it later," and hope that the child forgets.

It is important that parents and teachers try to expose children to the best children's books, recognizing that, like adults, they will frequently want other forms of literary entertainment. There is nothing wrong with romance novels, westerns, or spy novels; most of us enjoy holiday reading. And a dinner party would be horribly boring with guests who have read nothing but Kafka all their lives. We read all types of literature for all kinds of reasons. But I believe we must—as often as possible—set the highest standards for children.

Parents have it tougher than teachers in this regard. A teacher is supposed to maintain high standards. Teachers don't have four-, five-, and six-year-olds dragging them by the hand in the toy store to see a book they *must* have— children who won't stop whining, crying, and complaining until you buy it for them. (Teachers also have whining, crying, and complaining children, but they go home at the end of the day!) And teachers are with children in only one context—school. Schools have more controls. Parents are with children in a variety of situations and must interact with them in all of these.

I hope you don't feel like a rotten parent if your child has a collection of less than high quality books—Twinkies. While I'm the first to admit to being elitist and snooty about books, I am also full of contradictions. On my bookshelves at this very moment are hundreds of what I believe to be "good" children's books. I also own many books from my own childhood that I hold dear, and I consider it blasphemous for anyone to criticize them.Nevertheless, were I to evaluate them based on my present set of standards, they would not receive high marks. In addition, Nina (who you met in chapter 7) owns and adores some books that I would consider atrocious and would never recommend to anybody. The point is not to purge your home of these. Instead, do all you can to expose your child to the best quality literature most of the time.

When your child does read a book you consider less than ideal, don't murmur to yourself, "Well, at least he's reading something!" That's a rationalization that only encourages mediocre choices. Encourage all reading. And if your child falls in love with some junk-food books (as all children do), be pleasant, smile, and continue to do your best with other books.

Know also that a good children's book is rarely a hard sell. Choosing between a high quality book and a Twinkie is not the same to a child as choosing between spinach and a chocolate chip cookie. In spite of lapses into junk-food books, ninety-five percent of the books Nina enjoys are of high quality.

Writers and publishers want to publish books that children will enjoy, not books that they will avoid. The children's book market has never been better; thousands of new titles are published every year. While this is a tremendous asset, it is difficult to sift through many choices. The following are some guidelines to consider when searching for a good children's book, particularly for the pre-reading and beginning reading levels. These are the factors I consider whenever I look for new books in bookstores or libraries.

1. *Look for books with large type.* Children at the beginning reading level are learning about print. They must be able to see the words clearly. They must also see the spaces between words. While books with standard print should not be ignored, your child's library should contain books with larger type. Imagine if you were learning to read another language, and the print LOOKED LIKED THIS.

2. *Look for books with predictable language patterns.* This has already been detailed in the previous chapter. Although children will memorize all types of books if they hear them enough, books with predictable elements—repetition, rhythm, patterns, rhyme—gently and reassuringly help children commit the book to memory.

3. *Look for books with interesting content.* Well-written books, even those with only a few words on a page, have content. The stories are interesting and have identifiable characters. These books may include situations that allow the reader to reflect and examine his or her own life (insofar as a young child examines his

or her life). These books have intrigue, surprises. A book with content has "meat" in it—it has something to say. Pat Hutchins's counting book, *One Hunter,* for example, is a simple book, yet a marvelous example of how even books for beginning readers can have content. *One Hunter* tells the suspenseful, yet funny, story of a hunter stalking the jungle for wild animals. He passes blindly by each camouflaged animal until they all congregate together, and the hunter is frightened away. Each page states only the object: one hunter (page 1), two elephants (page 2), three monkeys (page 3), and so on. As simple as this story is, content is quite apparent. The reader understands something about the personality of the hunter. There is clearly a plot. The story has something to say.

4. *Look for books with quality illustrations.* As with all art forms, good illustration has an intangible element that touches us. Illustrators of children's books are masters of a sophisticated craft, most having studied art for many years and having dedicated their careers to this particular art form.

Children must be exposed to quality art just as they must be exposed to quality writing. Children respond to illustrations in books long before they notice the print. The illustrations tell the story. The child initially "reads" the book because of the illustrations. The art is the first provider of meaning. It is indeed a happy marriage of text and illustration that makes a successful picture book.

There is a difference between quality children's art and the kind of art that models cartoons and other popular children's television shows. Both are designed to sell a product, but I trust the integrity of the artist who is not trying to capitalize on the mesmerizing effects of children's TV programming.

5. *Know your child!* Many times I have made the mistake of buying wonderful books only to find children bored with my choices. The books were of the finest quality, but I had the wrong audience. Forcing a child to listen to or read a book simply because you spent $13.95 on it and it got a good review serves no purpose. Since you know your child, select books that he or she will probably find interesting.

6. *Avoid age restrictions.* Most good books are appreciated by children of various ages. Bryant was a child who entered kindergarten reading fluently. Handing him a book I thought that he would enjoy, he looked at me with tears in his eyes—Bryant cried a lot—and said, "I can't read this: it says 'for children seven and older,' and I'm only five."

It's important to remember the age of your child when choosing a book, but don't be afraid of choosing a book you feel is "above his age" or "below his age." I'm not certain what "above his age" and "below his age" mean anyway. There are five- and six-year-old children who love hearing novels. There are eleven- and twelve-year-olds who love listening to and looking at picture books.

7. *Try to choose a book that you enjoy too.* Children usually know if you don't like a book, and then reading is no pleasure for either of you. Of course, the term "disliking" does not mean that you hate it because you've read it 137 times. Even a saint would dislike

reading a book again and again—well, maybe not *every* book. But a book that I dislike the first time I read it usually does not get much better by the second, third, or fourth time. I will read it with little enthusiasm and voice inflection and will no doubt include a subliminal grumble throughout the reading that cannot help but influence the child's appreciation. Be honest with your child by saying, "Let's find a book we both like."

(For some specific book suggestions read "Special Books for Kids" on page 145.)

TWELVE

The School—Basals, Workbooks, and Other Myths of Learning

Having read this book to this point, you have some knowledge about how your child learns to read. You understand the role of prediction in reading, how phonics narrows the choices as you predict, how children improve their reading by the act of reading, and how reading aloud is the catalyst that creates this natural development of literacy.

Now we examine the worst case scenario:

With profound wisdom and great excitement, you take your child to the first day of kindergarten or grade one expecting the school to be similarly well-informed. You expect classroom reading activities to reflect the reading theory espoused in this book. You expect to see a classroom with a large selection of good children's books. You expect that the school day will include lots of time devoted to reading aloud and lots of independent reading.

Instead, what you see is your child presented with his or her first reading textbook. During a back-to-school night you hear about the "reading program" that the school uses. Your child's teacher states: "Our school uses XYZ basal reading series." You hear other statements such as, "We are eclectic. Of course we need to read aloud to children. That's important. But they need those reading skills too!" Kindergarten parents hear about the "letter of the week." Parents of first- and second-graders learn about the phonics program and about the wide range of reading levels of children in the classroom. You are informed that during the first two weeks of school, the reading specialist will test and evaluate your child's reading skills in order to place him or her in the appropriate reading group.

By the second day of school, your child begins to bring home completed workbook pages by the truckload, tells you in which reading group he or she has been placed and which story the group is reading. If you are lucky, you discover your child is in the "top" reading group, but you panic when you learn your child has been placed in the lowest group.

Disappointed, you recognize the stark contrast from what you thought you understood about reading and the one reality of the educational system: basal programs dominate most of today's educational scene. Basals are a series of books designed to teach and improve children's reading as they grow older. Reading in school is often limited to those particular books "taught" in a particular sequence.

Basal textbooks contain stories, poetry, and sometimes the text of songs. Each grade level has a designated text (or texts). Texts usually have a number indicating level of difficulty. For instance, a first-grade classroom might begin the year with a text called *Merrily We Roll Along*. That text is ranked "level 6." After students complete all the stories and activities in this text they advance to a level 7 first-grade text called *Happy Are the Clams*. The higher the number, the more sophisticated the reading. New reading skills are introduced at each level. Some grades have only one text for the entire year. Schools tend to adopt a single publisher's basal program to maintain continuity throughout the grades. Sometimes an entire school district will adopt a specific publisher's basal program so that children who transfer from one school to another within the district can fit in easily.

Basals tend to rank by number rather than grade level, partly in hopes that children will not know if they are reading "above grade level" or "below grade level." Different children in one classroom might read from a particular basal program at three or four different levels. This is why we so often hear about teachers who are frustrated by the number of reading groups or reading levels in the classroom. They feel unable to give enough of their time and attention to each.

Basals are a product of our society. We are a civilization of science that feels the need to operationalize each step of progress. We are uncomfortable with the intangible. We can chart the development of the light bulb, document each advancement of the space program, observe every working mechanism of a car. We base much learning theory upon rats running around mazes. We operate under the S-R rule—stimulus and response. We think of learning only as the accumulation of more and more facts.

We think of learning to read in the same way.

We want to see each and every step a child takes toward reading. We want to catch the mistakes, to help children avoid the pitfalls. We want to ensure that a child does not fall between the cracks when learning to read, and we feel reassured that a sequential reading program will help avoid this. We seem to function best when we feel in control.

Basals textbooks allow teachers, administrators, and parents to feel in control of a child's learning; that is to say, we think that if a child will follow the steps outlined in the teacher's manual, reading *will* occur. We are all convinced that we know the precise highway to the ultimate destination.

Unfortunately, this is all a myth. But myths have been at the heart of North America's reading programs for decades. Reading myths have inspired the multimillion dollar basal textbook industry. Textbook companies have perpetuated and sold these myths. Let's examine them more closely.

MYTH NUMBER ONE: *Reading instruction is systematic and sequential.*

Learning to read does not occur in tidy, orderly steps. Neither does learning to speak—a much more complex process. A child does not master language by first learning one word and then the next until the first 50,000 are learned. We do not "rank order" the learning of oral language. We don't say, "Now that Johnny has learned to speak all of these words he can move on to 'level 8' of learning to speak."

Neither did you sequentially learn all of the words you are reading now. I doubt you can remember the age or grade when you learned to read the word *sequentially*.

Sequential teaching and learning limits the reading material that children are capable of handling. Six-year-olds find words like *dinosaur, transformer,* or *Nintendo* recognizable because their meanings are important to them. They would not be considered "level 7 words." Words like *am, are,* or *the* are level 7 words because they are considered (by basal writers) to be easier for a six-year-old to learn.

Preschool and kindergarten children recognize each other's printed first names long before they recognize the words that basal programs include as important. Names are not "easy words." Some are short and some are long. Most are not even remotely phonetic. Classmates' names have strong meaning for children, and children learn to recognize those names for that reason. (Children's names, by the way, are not introduced in the order of difficulty—*Ann* before *Genevieve.*) There are many other "difficult" words that children recognize because they have power and meaning for them. Unfortunately, these words are not introduced until fifth or sixth grade, and sometimes not even then.

While it is reassuring to think of reading development as a sequential process of focusing first on parts of words, then on individual words; moving from simple to complex sentences; and then gradually and systematically acquiring more complex skills—and many educators strongly adhere to that position—others in the field of education do not view reading in this way at all.

I view reading as a form of language and know that all language learning occurs by doing the acts themselves: children learn to speak by speaking, to read by reading, and to write by writing. None of these can be learned in a manner that will ultimately be generalized and applied to real life if skills are taught in a prescribed timeline that has been developed by adults who presume that all children must learn the same skills in the same sequence.

Reading skills are acquired at the time the reader needs them. Knowledge and skills are experiential and are not learned in a linear fashion. Parents cannot sequence the order of their child's first spoken words. (Even though we hope their first words will be "Mama" or "Dada," we can't guarantee it.) Parents don't worry if a child pauses in the middle of a sentence when speaking instead of at the end. Parents don't worry about the ages at which their child uses interrogatory and exclamatory sentences. Children learn during the act of speaking, and they acquire more sophisticated oral language skills when they feel that they are necessary. But when the form of language is print, many parents worry tremendously about children learning these same skills in a particular order. It isn't necessary. They will learn them in exactly the same way as they did when learning to speak.

MYTH NUMBER TWO: *Children must be taught a defined series of skills, including phonics, structural analysis, and sight words, which become progressively more sophisticated. Each new skill must be mastered before the next skill is learned.*

Breaking down learning into various skills does not allow children to learn meaningfully and relevantly; and breaking learning down into its component parts before children see the whole picture makes learning extremely difficult and frustrating. Children cannot see the parts before they see the whole. Imagine putting together a jigsaw puzzle without first seeing the picture on the box. Then suppose you had to place each piece correctly before the next puzzle piece was handed to you, and this continued until all one thousand pieces were placed correctly. Do you think anyone would succeed? And even if someone did, how enjoyable would it have been?

While baseball players spend time developing the skills of batting, pitching, or sliding, the foundation of those skills is laid during the hundreds of times the game is played. No sports person I know was introduced to the game through the isolated development of a particular skill. The first time very young children are introduced to baseball, they are taught to swing at the ball and run. There is immediate purpose in the action. Later on, after some confidence and abilities are developed, specific skills are refined, but then always applied directly and immediately to a real-life playing situation.

Basal programs usually demand that children learn and practice skills *before* they are ever expected to use them. A fifth-grade child might be taught about prefixes, then provided with a workbook page that requires matching all the prefixes in one column with the appropriate root words in a second column. Only after this is the child encouraged to read a story (written or chosen with plenty of prefixes to "reinforce" the lesson taught). The same is true for a beginning reader. The traditional rule in basal programs is: learn the skill, *then* practice it.

Learning occurs best, however, when there is an immediate purpose behind it, and the skills are practiced during the experience. You don't learn to bake a cake by first practicing to separate eggs. You become better at separating eggs the more you bake cakes. A child will understand, pronounce, and recognize spaghetti by having it for dinner, not by practicing the pronunciation of the word *spaghetti* or studying its picture before seeing or tasting it. The mastery of skills occurs during the practice.

In some programs, basal texts may require children to recognize words by sight. The introduction of sight words is carefully controlled. "Harder" sight words are sequentially introduced at higher levels. In basal lingo, this is known as a "controlled vocabulary." There are problems with this. Teaching children to say words by sight, out of context, does not mean they will be able to read them in the context of a story. Some recent basal programs that include "quality literature" have edited these stories to maintain a controlled vocabulary. Here, words are changed and deleted so that stories are "easier" for children to read. What would be left of the Bible's "Genesis" if words like *beginning, created,* and *heaven* were considered too difficult, and simpler words were substituted: *At the start of the world, God made the sky . . . .*

Finally, fluent readers do not focus on the *parts* of written language. As has been said many times in this book, fluent readers—both children and adults—focus on the *meanings* of written language. Fluent readers intuitively know that the meanings of stories are much more important than the words. Fluent readers will either guess what an unknown word is or skip the word altogether. They get the meaning of the sentence without it. I've known many young readers who love reading *Tom Sawyer* or *Huckleberry Finn* even though they are not able to read every word.

"Word attack skills" result from predicting what the word might be, based on the meaning of the story—not because the reader understands what a prefix is.

MYTH NUMBER THREE: *Most, if not all, learning to read can be accomplished through the basal reader.*

All basals contain a finite number of stories, songs, or poems. It is a preposterous assumption that all, or even some, of these stories would gain the attention and interest of all, or even most, children. Children need exposure to a large quantity and variety of books, far more than even the most sophisticated basal series could include.

Children choose books in the same way that adults do. We enjoy books that are personally relevant and interesting. We become fans of one or two particular authors; we become fond of certain genres. We become interested in a subject and read about it. We may read the same book two or three times in our lives because it moves us. Children do precisely the same thing.

Basal publishers cannot accommodate the infinite number of reasons that children read, nor can they assume to cover their many differing interests. This is one reason that most learning cannot be accomplished through the basal reader.

Most people reading this book probably think that they learned to read from basal readers. Our childhood memories are rather selective, and formal activities done in school can overshadow the more important informal activities that teachers and parents do that truly create an environment for literacy.

You learned to read in a multitude of ways. Hearing a large variety of meaningful books read aloud was certainly one of the most significant.

MYTH NUMBER FOUR: *Children need practice and reinforcement of material and skills taught. Workbooks that correspond to these skills should be provided so that children master these skills.*

Children must practice their reading regularly. But what type of practice is most appropriate? Workbooks are a common form of practice in this country, with most children spending much of their school time practicing in workbooks.

A workbook is a consumable paperback that is part of a basal program. ("Consumable" means that the pages of the book are to be written on by the child, making the book unusable by others.) Workbooks also come in the form of skill sheets, dittos, and activity packs. When children use their workbooks (which correspond in level of difficulty with the basal reader), they practice a skill that usually has been taught by the teacher. The skills are varied and plentiful. And each reading skill needs one or more workbook pages for children to practice.

I wish I had a dollar for every workbook sold in this country. They are not only used in schools, but are also made available to parents in toy stores, book stores, and grocery stores. They promise to "reinforce your child's reading skills," "prepare your child for reading," "develop comprehension skills," or "teach phonics." Textbook publishers might even promise world peace if they thought it could be circled, underlined, or crossed out—the primary activity of workbooks.

Look at the examples of workbook pages shown on pages 105–106. Notice what these workbook pages ask children to do: "draw a line . . . ," "draw a ring around the word . . . ," "color the pictures . . . ," "put an *x* next to the

1 Say each picture name.
2 Listen to the first sound.
3 Color the picture if its name begins with the sound of g.

Introducing the conson

Workbook Samples

Draw a line from each picture to the correct word.

hen

goat

men

boat

pen

28

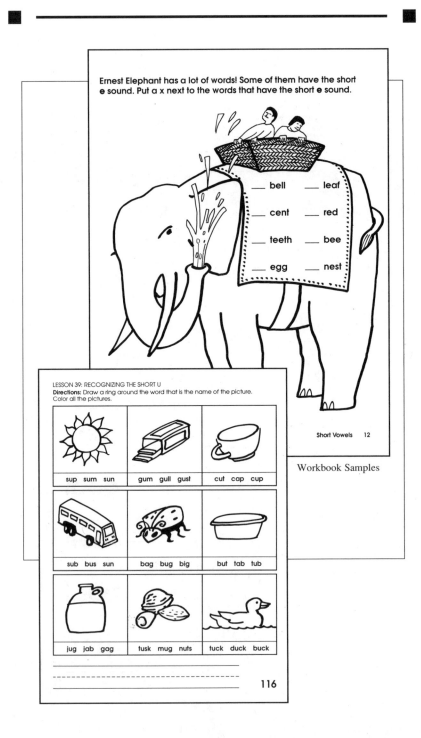

Ernest Elephant has a lot of words! Some of them have the short e sound. Put a x next to the words that have the short e sound.

____ bell   ____ leaf

____ cent   ____ red

____ teeth   ____ bee

____ egg   ____ nest

Short Vowels   12

Workbook Samples

LESSON 39: RECOGNIZING THE SHORT U
Directions: Draw a ring around the word that is the name of the picture.
Color all the pictures.

sup sum sun	gum gull gust	cut cap cup
sub bus sun	bag bug big	but tab tub
jug jab gag	tusk mug nuts	tuck duck buck

116

words . . . ." Others ask children to do such tasks as cut and paste a word, underline the prefix. Children are practicing geometric shapes and small motor coordination more than practicing reading.

Most workbooks do not benefit the children but instead benefit (1) publishers, who each year make millions of dollars on their sale; (2) teachers, who use workbooks as "seat work" so children will stay quiet; (3) schools, who point to the quantity of work children do in a day; (4) parents, who decorate their walls and refrigerators with a multitude of papers; and (5) stamp companies, who manufacture stamps reading *good work, great job, terrific,* or *messy, do again.*

Workbooks do not benefit children's learning.

Workbooks do little if anything to help children learn to read. Imagine if I were a cooking instructor and my first lesson was "How to make an apple pie." I hand the class their apple pie workbook page and provide the following instructions: "Circle the apples . . . underline the rolling pin . . . draw a line to the sugar . . . match the pastry with the pie tin." I do not think many students would then know how to make a pie, even if they practiced this page a thousand times.

We teach children to play sports by playing sports with them. Children learn to sew by sewing. We teach children dance and gymnastics by having them dance and tumble. We teach children to read by having them circle items on workbook pages?

There are many other reasons I don't like workbooks: They are often confusing, they are boring, they are horribly uncreative, and they focus on one "right answer" when children must learn that a problem can often have many solutions.

Clearly, there are some children who enjoy workbooks. Children who find them easy enjoy them because they are good at them. But there is very little thinking or learning involved. Their completion is a simple mechanical process.

There are other children who do not find workbook completion as easy as the first group, but figure out the workbook system quickly enough to fake their way through the pages to receive adequate marks. Like the first group, these children think that they are learning from workbooks but learn in spite of them.

There are, however, a multitude of children who cannot do workbook pages. These children are frustrated by them; they tear these papers with all their erasing, sometimes rip their pages out of anger, give up, feel stupid or like failures, and often become behavior problems. They, too, think learning is supposed to result from all their circling and underlining. Because they don't feel they're learning, these children find other ways to get attention, to feel important. These children learn how to cheat. They feel they *must* to keep up with the rest of the class. They don't realize that they are really learning no less than the others.

A workbook is a test. If you can do a test easily there is no need for it; if you can't do the test easily, you need to find more meaningful ways to practice. And parents need to find more imaginative ways of decorating walls and refrigerators.

I have spent a great deal of time discussing basal textbooks and their accompanying workbooks because so many parents expect their children to use them. Parents spend a substantial amount of time worrying that their child is reading at the appropriate level. Parents spend a lot of time comparing one child's level with another child's level.

My hope is that parents will understand the liabilities associated with basals in the classroom and will support those teachers who are willing to teach reading without them. I hope that parents will question teachers who expect young children to spend many hours each day filling out workbook pages. Parents must believe their children when they complain about workbooks being hard, confusing, or boring. Parents must empathize with children with homework assignments that involve drawing lines between syllables or circling all the *the*'s, *on*'s, and *at*'s.

I hope parents are vocal about the kinds of activities that schools use to pit one child against another. (Basals, by their very nature, promote tremendous competition: "I'm on level 7, and you're only on level 5!") Try not to worry if your child isn't at the highest basal level of the classroom.

To be fair, some textbooks companies have written better basals than others. Some include unaltered good literature; some provide references to other sources; some provide better workbooks. This is due in part to the disdain of an increasing number of teachers toward traditional reading textbooks and the linear hierarchy of reading instruction. Many of this group of teachers would like to do away with basals altogether, but this is easier said than done. The security that basals provide leads to a tremendous amount of anxiety from teachers who have used them for years and who are threatened with their removal.

Additionally, many teachers who wish to rid themselves of basals face supportive colleagues, but run into opposition from the school principal, the reading specialist, the district reading coordinator, or you, the parent.

Frequently the parent is the most fearsome of the lot. Parents, unknowingly, perpetuate the "myths of learning" by asking what the basal reading program is for that year, by demanding information on their child's rank in the class, by insisting on more worksheets for homework, by evaluating good teaching on a teacher's knowledge of all the reading skills their child does or does not possess, by criticizing teachers when they allow children to choose books that are interesting and relevant to them. The list can go on and on.

A parent can be intimidating to a teacher. A parent can also be very supportive. This is not a plea to divorce yourself from your child's education. On the contrary, your questions and concerns, which the teacher may find intimidating, actually indicate your concern and care for your child's education.

Consider these questions and comments that demonstrate your new-found knowledge and wisdom about the reading process:

- Must my child use a basal? I'd prefer him [her] to choose books that he [she] will enjoy because they are interesting and relevant.

- My child seems to be spending much of his [her] time filling out workbook pages. Are there any more meaningful activities he [she] can do?

- Thank you for letting me know that my child is in the high reading group. However, I think that *all* members of the classroom have something to contribute to his [her] learning and wonder if there will be lots of opportunities for him [her] to interact with others.

- I'm certain you're working hard to help my child improve his [her] reading, but I really hope that you will make sure that he [she] will spend much more time reading books than practicing skills.

If you get responses such as, "I have to use the basal, they (meaning the school/principal/district) require it," don't take this for an answer. Politely ask, "Who can I speak with about this?" Sometimes no one is quite certain who "they" are, so be persistent. Involve other parents in this process.

And if your child has a teacher who is not using a basal; who lets and helps children choose the books they want to read; who runs a classroom in which there is a tremendous amount of sharing, interaction, and collaboration; who doesn't believe in fragmenting reading into isolated bits; who doesn't seem to care much about a child's deficiencies, errors, or mistakes but maximizes a child's strengths; who makes every child, no matter how "low," feel as though he or she can read; and who, at back-to-school-night, sounds knowledgeable about reading theory and avoids hiding behind a reading program (and who does not spend seventy-five percent of the evening discussing discipline and grading procedures)—who may be the only teacher in the school teaching this way and is scared to death when you want to conference so has postponed the conference three times because of "a sudden string of deaths in the family"—corner that teacher just before lunch and say:

"I just want you to know that I am so thrilled my child is in your classroom. I want you to know that I am not worried about reading skills, grade level, basals, and workbooks. Keep up the good work!"

This last comment will either give him or her the best lunch hour he or she has had in a long time, or cause an anxiety attack precipitated by disbelief.

It's worth the risk.

THIRTEEN

Looking for the Right Classroom

Literacy begins at home and then extends to school. Your new knowledge of literacy development will allow you to observe classroom reading activities with more information, sophistication, and understanding. You can now begin to assess whether or not a school and/or classroom will provide the kind of literary environment that you want for your child. In any one school there are often several approaches to literacy. It's up to you to decide which approach you prefer, and to live with what is available.

Parents with options for schooling search for the "perfect school." They look for an environment that will provide their child with a positive learning experience, where their child will learn with enthusiasm, discover inner peace, as well as learn reading and mathematics. Unfortunately, finding the perfect learning environment is like looking for the perfect relationship or being the perfect parent—it just doesn't exist. Some teachers are more skilled than others; some programs are better than others; some schools promise to serve children with special needs—learning handicapped, gifted, and so on. Some schools are established specifically to meet special needs and interests.

Ultimately, all schools have good and bad features, advantages and disadvantages.

I believe that certain features should exist in all classrooms. Since this book is about reading, my comments are limited to that aspect of the curriculum. However, there is relevancy to all areas.

1. I look for a classroom where the reading program consists primarily of children reading good books. These books are easily and frequently accessible to children, and there is a large degree of personal choice. In the early grades, I hope to see many enlarged books (commonly referred to as "big books") used in the classroom.

2. I look for a classroom where basal and accompanying workbooks, worksheets, and dittos are not the essence of the reading program. I am concerned when I see children sit quietly at their desks filling out these activity sheets.

3. I look for a classroom that does not emphasize the formal teaching of phonics. I am uncomfortable when children are grouped for long bouts of reading phonetically written materials intended for phonics instruction. I am unhappy learning that the classroom or school's philosophy is "first have them learn their phonics, then they can begin reading literature."

4. I look for a classroom where reading is a social activity, where there is a lot of interaction between children. This means a noisy classroom. I feel uncomfortable when children are instructed to work silently

and told, "Do your own work. Don't help your neighbors." I love seeing classrooms where small and large groups of children work, talk, and explore together.

5. I look for a classroom in which children make lots of errors while reading and no one, not even the teacher, panics about it. The teacher tells me that errors are essential for learning, and may tell me that formal and informal assessments of those "errors" indicate that they are sensible ones. The teacher demonstrates awareness of each child's reading strategies and offers support and guidance to those children who need further strategies.

6. I look for a classroom free from reading tests. I know that it is unrealistic to expect schools to eliminate state- or province-wide testing altogether (though I will celebrate the day this occurs). What I refer to here is the myriad of weekly testing, end-of-unit testing, end-of-book testing, criteria testing, placement testing, and so on. Messages children receive from these tests include: "I am dumber than everyone," "I am smarter than everyone," "I'm a failure," "I don't know anything," or even "Cheating is the only way I'll pass."

7. I look for a classroom where reading is not competitive. Children learn best in environments that encourage cooperation and collaboration. The more competitive the environment, the less children learn. Competition also encourages a preoccupation with correctness, cheating, and failure.

8. I look for a classroom that does not break reading into parts. This not only includes the sequence of skills described in chapter 12 but also the division of reading

into incomprehensible subject matters. The most confusing to me has always been the difference between "Reading" and "Language." Teachers have tried to explain it to me, but I still don't understand the difference unless they mean that "language" sometimes includes grammar. Reading *is* language.

9. I look for a classroom where reading is both a pleasurable activity and a tool of learning. Even beginning readers should "read to learn" (in contrast to "learn to read"). In the process of reading to learn, children *do* learn to read. Reading must be done for its own sake, but reading also allows us to study various aspects of life, so I look for a teacher who doesn't fragment the day into "reading time" and "social studies time" and "science time." All of these content areas should be integrated throughout the day.

10. I look for a classroom that seldom groups children according to their reading abilities. I look for a teacher who knows that every member of a classroom has something to contribute to the others, regardless of their reading levels. The teacher periodically brings together children who need similar strategies without making them feel labeled.

As I reread my "top 10 list," I cannot help but reflect on the limited number of classrooms in which all these factors occur all of the time. The numbers are small but growing. But since it is still rare to witness all ten components, it might be useful to apply the same kinds of standards that magazines use when they offer self-help examination or compatibility tests. A *yes* to each positive factor on the top 10 list counts as one. Here is the scale:

0   Hmm. Have you considered home schooling?

1–2   Give a copy of this book to the teacher, and be thankful that your child is not in the classroom down the hallway, which is even worse.

3–5   Give a copy of this book to the teacher, and be very supportive since this teacher is probably just beginning to make a transition.

6–8   Give a copy of this book to the teacher as it will reinforce a great majority of his or her classroom reading activities.

9–10 The teacher probably lent you a copy of this book, so get a copy for yourself and share it with other parents. Be thrilled that your child is getting this kind of education for at least one year and know that, unless your child is enrolled in a school dedicated to this type of teaching, it may not occur again for several more years.

Finally, since many parents reading this book have a child who will soon enter kindergarten, here is a special note just for you (although parents of first-grade children might also read this).

This is a very exciting time. It is also a very anxiety-provoking time. After all, you may think of kindergarten as "real school." You may consider your child's kindergarten experience as preparation for Harvard.

I have never found a way to completely reassure parents about their child's formal reading instruction (in contrast to their informal reading instruction, which began at birth). It just isn't true to say: "It's not that important. There are many other years that can make up for a poor beginning." Kindergarten and grade one are critical years in a child's life. A child's formalized beginning-reading experience may determine that child's future reading success. The strongest teachers must bring their knowledge and talents to those early grades. A good kindergarten and first-grade experience is essential, but one person's good experience is not necessarily another's.

By now, the reader of this book knows my biases. I don't believe that a good kindergarten is one in which children are expected to read by June. I am not impressed by this, no matter how much a school may flaunt its test results.

I don't think a good kindergarten is one in which a child can sound out words or recognize words by sight. I don't think a good kindergarten teacher permanently groups children according to "academic abilities." I don't think a good kindergarten is one that replicates a younger version of first grade.

I witness more and more academically demanding kindergartens. In my local area, I know of two schools in upper middle-class neighborhoods where the kindergarten expectations are so high that over half the children enter kindergarten a year older (at age six) than those in other kindergartens. Kindergarten children in these schools are expected to read by the end of the year. The average five- or six-year-old cannot handle this pressure, expectation, and, yes, exploitation, but these schools are honored by local school officials, parents, and even government as outstanding educational environments.

I don't believe this is what kindergarten is about.

A good kindergarten provides an environment in which children are filled with the language of literature, song, and poetry. Kindergarten children must hear literature read aloud, learn old and new songs, dance, dramatize, and be in an environment where print makes sense. Kindergarten children are in school to understand themselves, the world around them, and how they fit into that world.

The process by which a child learns to read is as important as the reading itself—perhaps even more important. The school reading program must focus on making reading meaningful and relevant and must provide even young readers with the sense of "owning" their own learning—making them feel that they are in charge of the process of learning.

My more effusive teacher friends want reading and schooling to be fun for children. They want children to love school and enjoy learning. While I understand this desire, it is surprisingly not my foremost goal as a classroom teacher. I want reading to be seen by children as meaningful, relevant, and purposeful. Ultimately, the affective by-products of having fun, loving school, and enjoying learning will result.

FOURTEEN
Questions and Answers

Q. *Don't the illustrations in books distract children from learning to read?*

A. Absolutely not. In fact, illustrations play a critical role in the reading process. When they listen to a story, children must make a connection between their own personal world (experiences) and the language of that story. Illustrations help connect the meaning of the story to the child's own experiences. That bridge allows for enjoyment and for comprehension. When children are first learning to read they need to have that immediate visual image in front of them. Later on, after they have heard a particular story many times, children will use the illustrations as prompts or cues to rehearse the story. Finally, after many experiences, children construct those visual cues in their minds (imaginary illustrations). This is what adults do when they read "adult" books. (And let's not forget that illustrations are visually and aesthetically appealing.)

Q. *My child doesn't really read books, he just memorizes them, doesn't he?*

A. Yes, but that's exactly what *should* happen. Memorizing books is one of the first steps in learning to read. The memorization of a book's exact words is preceded by storing the *meaning* of the story inside the child's head. When listening to the story read aloud, the child never paid attention to the words of the story; the child paid attention to the story's meaning. That is why, when first retelling the story, the child's replication is not exact. It's not like an actor memorizing the words of a play. The more the story is heard, however, the more familiar are the words; the more familiar the words, the more exact is the replication; the more exact the replication, the more the child repeats familiar passages when parents read aloud; the more the child repeats passages orally, the more the child focuses on the words of that passage and finally reads in the traditional sense. All of this comes out of "just memorizing." Learning to read naturally occurs in this way.

Q. *The preschool teacher keeps talking about reading readiness. What does this mean, and do you think it's necessary?*

A. Historically, reading readiness meant that before children could read, they had to be mentally prepared. They were assigned tasks for that preparation. One skill to be refined was "visual discrimination." The theory was that a child must learn to discriminate between words, especially physically similar words (*was* and *saw*, for example). Since children were unable to deal with print, they were given visual discrimination tasks that usually involved doing something with geometric shapes.

These tasks grew increasingly sophisticated. Children had to match unfamiliar shapes in the same way. This led ultimately to matching words: *Look at the word in the shaded box. Then mark the other box that has the same word in it:*

Reading readiness also involved "auditory discrimination," knowledge of the alphabet and of vocabulary.

If you have read this book up to now, you know my opinion of these kinds of activities. Children "read" long before formal schooling. Readiness involves immersing them in literature, not circle-the-box tasks.

Q. *Do you advocate reading only literature with predictable language patterns to children?*

A. No. Children must hear all kinds of literature and can memorize all kinds of literature, although young children who are learning to read do enjoy literature that contains repetitive elements. I am always reminded, however, of Nina at three and how she loved a *Big Bird Sesame Street* book. This book was lengthy, each page containing many words. There was no repetition in this book. But Nina had heard the book a thousand times. I sat down with Nina once and listened to her "read" this book aloud. She had memorized it verbatim. She made almost no errors in her retelling. This is a good example of a child who was read to from a book without patterned language, yet she memorized it. Read all types of literature to your child.

Q. *My four-year-old so badly wants to read. Doesn't it make sense to try to help him?*

A. If he sits on your lap and hears "old favorites," again and again, particularly the predictable types mentioned earlier, I have little doubt that your child will feel like a reader, even if he can't recognize the words. You must send an unspoken message to your child that your definition of reading includes "reading the pictures" and must not distinguish that from reading the words. The children who proudly read the pictures don't feel that they "so badly want to read" because they already believe they can. Parents must be very cautious not to send signals that reading is "recognizing the words" or to distinguish between reading at home and what will occur in school. For example, the parent who says to a four-year-old, "Tomorrow you will start kindergarten and learn to read," sends a message to the child that all the reading he has done up to that point in his life has *not* been reading.

It is possible that some of the pressure to read is self-imposed. If it is, then you can only be as relaxed about it as possible, for surely this child is driven in many other aspects of life. However, I think that few children are born genetically predisposed to want to read before they are five. And those four-year-olds who do want to read may have parents who place prime importance on early reading and unwittingly send this message to their child.

The information in this book is not designed to "get children to read earlier." First of all, that's impossible. Learning to read naturally means exactly that—allowing children to come into reading as naturally as learning to speak. It can't be hurried or forced. Reading to your child should not be part of an incentive plan for the purpose of offering hope that someday soon "you will be able to read all by yourself." There is a message in that statement that can allow a child to respond, "But what if I *can't* learn to do it myself?"

For many years parents have read to their children for the sheer joy of the relationship between parent and child. But other important learning factors developed in children at the same time: a love of books, knowledge about print, and an understanding of the language of literature.

Q. *Do you think that children should be accountable for every book they read?*

A. As a teacher, I want to be aware of which and how many books a child is reading, but many schools carry this to such an extreme that a child can't read a book without having to report on it. Schools spend so much time making children accountable that they forget why they are in school in the first place. Then there are the book-report forms that children are asked to complete, which are boring and ridiculous. No wonder so many children have lost the joy of reading. How would you feel if you had to report on every book you read?

Q. *What do you think of rewards to encourage children's reading?*

A. I am absolutely opposed to contests, stars, stickers, or any other rewards for reading books. Would anyone consider a contest to determine who watched the most television or who went to the most movies? Of course not. Because they are meaningful to them, children don't need bribes for these activities. If children are presented with literature from the time that they are infants, motivation to read becomes internal—not external. The media also encourages children to read. While well-intended and probably effective, it's too bad that children must be encouraged to read in this way. We shouldn't need bribes or celebrities to encourage children to pick up books.

Q. *What exactly do you mean by "reading for meaning"?*

A. When a child responds to directions such as, "Clean up your mess," or "Put the toys on the table," the child pays attention to the ideas being communicated. If you ask a child to define the individual words spoken, it is unlikely that he or she would be able to tell you what *up* or *put* meant. Children learning oral language respond to the meanings. When children—or adults— read, they do not respond to the individual words either. They respond to the meaning, the ideas, the sense of what the author is trying to say. Readers who pay attention to individual words lose the meaning. Try to focus on each word or sound spoken when you have a conversation with someone. You'll soon realize that it is impossible to respond to the speaker because you have lost the meaning.

Q. *Is "meaning" the same as "comprehension skills"?*

A. I don't like the term "comprehension skills" because it makes me think of children reading three or four paragraphs to answer seven questions that somebody else thinks are important. It also implies that comprehension is a separate skill from reading. It is not.

"Comprehension" also implies that the author has ideas that the reader must understand, independent of the reader's background. Meaning is more complex. Meaning involves the reader's background, experiences, ideas, and beliefs interacting with the story. No two readers ever interpret a story exactly the same way. Fascinating, isn't it?

Q. *Your last answer makes me nervous. I certainly hope that when my surgeon reads how to perform my surgery next week, he [she] won't "interpret" the procedure.*

A. And I certainly hope that your surgeon has had many many hands-on surgical experiences prior to reading the manual, experiences that will enable him [her] to bring to that reading a greater depth of understanding than someone who has just picked up the book.

It is true that when preparing to read factual material the reader adopts a different stance than when reading for pleasure. When reading an encyclopedia, my goal is to take away specific information. When reading a novel, my goal is the reading experience itself. Unfortunately, many classrooms apply an informational reading position for pleasure reading. Most of the literature young children read is for pleasure, and should be left for both personal reflection and appreciation.

Q. *Aren't sight words helpful?*

A. Yes, recognition of words by sight is very useful. Your ability to read this book is due in part to your sight-word knowledge. My objection is to teaching words in isolation. Children begin to recognize basic sight vocabulary by first "reading" books they already know. They see these words again and again within a meaningful context. If seen enough, children will come to recognize these words in a variety of contexts. If a child doesn't recognize a "basic sight word" in isolation, this is probably because the word hasn't occurred enough in his or her reading to commit it to memory. This is true for adults too. There are probably words that you cannot remember how to read or spell because you haven't seen them often enough. However, if a word is important enough, and you read or write it often enough, you will remember it.

Q. *Don't you believe that children need to be taught skills?*

A. The moment someone says "skills," the implication is teaching children how to sound out words. I prefer to think that children need many more reading strategies than sounding-out skills. (I address various strategies in another question.) Assuming that there are skills to be learned, isn't it better to teach those skills at the moment of need rather than because someone has determined that a particular skill should be taught at a specified grade level? If a skill is taught when the child needs to apply it, the teaching will most likely occur only once because it will be learned. But a skill taught in isolation, before it is necessary, may need to be retaught hundreds of times. Even then, it won't "stick" unless it is needed. Skills must not take precedence over meaning.

Q. *I learned to read phonetically. Since this method was good enough for me, why isn't it good enough for my child?*

A. Children learn to read even when their introduction to the subject is poor. This is a tribute to the brain, not a tribute to the approach. Those children who learned to read fluently in schools that used the phonics-first approach fortunately had been given good introduction to literacy before their formal education. While no irreparable harm was done there were many missed opportunities for these children—their backgrounds in literacy were not enhanced. I believe that children who do not have literate backgrounds are hindered by phonetic approaches.

Q. *But the phonics approach works for some children, doesn't it?*

A. No. Adults think that the phonics approach works because they already know how to read. Once you know how to read, phonics makes perfect sense.

Q. *Doesn't phonics help in word recognition?*

A. Yes, but you must first have some sense of what the word might be. Sometimes I will tell children who come to a word that they don't know to guess what the word might be, then look at the first letter or two to see if one of their choices fits, and then confirm their guess by looking at the last letter of the word.

Q. *Don't all children learn differently? Some children do seem to learn best through phonics.*

A. This is a very common, but loaded, question. To deny this statement suggests that I ignore individual difference among children. First, I will repeat that phonics is one part of a reading "cueing" system. A teacher who ignores phonics as one reading strategy is, in my opinion, ignoring part of reading. It is the isolated, systematic approach to phonics teaching that I object to. *All* children need a variety of strategies to help them read. Focusing on only one system, whatever that may be, does not make sense.

Reading is like a game of twenty questions. The more sophisticated the questions, the more likely you are to guess the answer. When I taught kindergarten I put a surprise inside a box and asked children for questions that would give them hints. Most kindergarten children asked lower level questions such as: "Is it a ball?" "Is it a dog?" "Is it a . . . ?" These questions provided little information. Learning to ask higher level questions such as "Is it something to eat?" "Is it alive?" "Is it heavy?" "Does it grow?" helped them to arrive at the answer—to analyze the situation—more efficiently.

Proficient readers ask the equivalent of higher level questions as they read, and they've learned to ask those questions from the beginning of their literacy development. That is why it is simplistic to say that all children learn differently. It's not either/or. Phonics, or sounding out words, is akin to asking lower level questions. It's the least useful strategy, but it *is* a strategy. Examples of higher level reading strategies that children can use are: determining what makes sense in the context, what sounds like language, what the picture shows; deciding to skip the word because you can't figure it out; stopping in mid-sentence and rereading the sentence. These are only a few of many other strategies. All children need to call upon a variety of strategies depending on the situation, just as all parents need a variety of higher-level discipline strategies to deal with a child who misbehaves. If those higher level discipline strategies break down, parents resort to lower level ones such as . . . (you fill in the blank). It's usually not a permanent solution, but it gets you through the moment.

For goodness sake, don't allow yourself to be overwhelmed by all this educational talk about reading strategies. You help your child with a very common reading strategy. "What's *this* word?" your child asks. You answer. It's not a high level strategy, but it's an important one.

Q. *My child has a reading problem. Would phonics help her?*

A. Often a child who has "learning problems" in reading is offered remedial help. There are a variety of approaches to remediation and one approach is increased phonics. I do not believe this to be an appropriate tool. Often, those children who have trouble reading have difficulty because their formal introduction was phonics. Providing the same confusing activities for a confused child, individually or in a small group, doesn't help matters; it only makes them worse. Children having trouble reading usually need the exact opposite of a phonetic approach. They need an approach that parallels the early experiences of children who emerge naturally into literacy.

Q. *Does everyone agree with what you have said about literacy development?*

A. Of course not. But there is *universal agreement* that reading aloud to your child from a very young age is critically important, and that you need to talk with your child and provide meaningful experiences for him or her. There is *general agreement* that workbooks of old were not much good. There is *moderate agreement* that basals of old weren't good, and there is *general disagreement* about the new basal textbooks—many feel they are important and useful; many do not. There is *no real disagreement* that children must know some phonics, but there is *tremendous disagreement* on how phonics is learned and applied. One side insists that at least in the early grades, classrooms should have some formal, sequential presentation of phonics. The other side says that the acquisition of phonics cannot be taught formally and sequentially and that children actively construct their phonetic knowledge through the acts of reading and writing. Some of you reading this at this very moment will immediately agree with the first side. By now all of you know that I side with the other.

Q. *But what does the research say?*

A. Research has been, is, and will forever be in dispute for one major reason: one's philosophical perspective shapes the tools of evaluation, the methodology of evaluation, and the goals of evaluation. Educational research reminds me very much of psychological research. Will psychoanalysts and behaviorists ever agree on psychotherapy techniques? Each perspective approaches mental health differently. Each has a different opinion of growth and change. Each evaluates clients differently. In the same way, reading researchers debate the teaching of reading with each side's evaluations based on their own criteria and standards. So, to answer your question specifically, the research that I believe is most credible justifies this philosophy.

Q. *I believe what you have to say about learning to read, but my child's kindergarten classroom emphasizes phonics. What should I do?*

A. You can continue to read to your child. Hopefully, all that you have provided up to now will allow your child to transcend a skills-based classroom. Keep instilling the love of literature and the idea that books contain meaning. This is precisely what happened to me going through school. Fortunately, I had a dedicated mother who continued to read to me. I struggled through school but continued to read at home. This is not to say that there were no scars as a result, but it could have been much worse. A parent once told me how her five-year-old entered kindergarten reading fluently and was immediately placed in a reading group that taught the sounds. "Why are you doing this?" his mother asked. "He can read already!" The teacher responded, "He doesn't know his individual sounds." "But he can read!" the mother stated once again. The teacher was just as determined: "He needs to learn his sounds." This may not happen in every classroom, but I have heard this tale more than once. It is very sad. I have seen children enter kindergarten on the verge of reading, have phonics thrust upon them, and actually reverse their reading enthusiasm and abilities. These children are now totally hung up on saying every word correctly.

Q. *My child's teacher is using a publisher's literature-based reading program. What do you think of this kind of program?*

A. I think that, for the most part, these programs are an improvement over the basals of the past. Some are better than others. Several publishers include very good stories in their programs. Certainly, if I were forced to choose between my child reading from one of these programs over a traditional basal program, I'd choose the former. However, this is like asking which of two movies that I didn't like I would prefer to see again. The answer is neither. But basal textbooks are as much a part of North American society as Mom and apple pie. To think that the vast majority of schools will do away with them is a fantasy, albeit a pleasant one. The current addition of literature in basal programs is the result of the increasingly strong push for literature as an integral part of classrooms.

There is much talk about the "basalization of literature," which perpetuates many of the flaws of more traditional basal programs: atrocious worksheets often accompany good literature; certain books are designated for—and limited to—particular grade levels; stories are sometimes changed to make them easier for the children.

Despite good literature appearing in many of these programs, they are frequently used liked basals of old. And what's the result? For the past twenty years, as a result of instructional methods, children have learned to hate reading. Now, if we're not careful, they'll learn to hate literature.

Q. *Don't you think you're hard on basals?*

A. No.

Q. *My child loves workbooks and feels disappointed when they aren't used. Are they really so bad?*

A. Children who like workbooks feel this way because they are good at them, find them easy, and are not required to think critically. Many children want workbooks because they think they are supposed to have them. They see older students, older brothers and sisters, or neighborhood children using them. Children and parents like workbooks because they are perceptible evidence of something occurring in school (workbooks can often be the only tangible evidence of learning in the classroom). There are many more effective tangible items that children can bring home. Charlotte Schell, one of the most gifted teachers I know, once said the most important thing that children can bring home is themselves.

Q. *My six-year-old daughter is in the kind of ideal classroom you describe, but she will be in a very traditional classroom next year. Shouldn't her first-grade teacher do some traditional kind of work to prepare her for the next year?*

A. I have a friend whose sister is mildly retarded and suffers from cerebral palsy. This girl's family certainly did not spend the first five years of this child's life calling her "spaz" and "retarded" to prepare her for what she would hear when she went to school. Her family provided her with a foundation of love, acceptance, and caring, and that is what prepared her for the name-calling she heard when she first entered school. We must not provide bad education to prepare children for bad education. We must provide children with good education, and *that* will prepare them for bad education.

Q. *I hear a lot of talk about "whole language" at my child's school. Is this a new program?*

A. All this whole language talk is confusing for everybody, including teachers. I'm not surprised. Whole language is *not* a program. It is a theory of and approach to literacy development that has been discussed and written about since the early 1960s by a host of influential educators, most notably by Kenneth Goodman and Frank Smith. They discussed the notion that children, given the appropriate classroom environment, will learn to read in the same manner that they learned to speak.

The practical classroom implementation of whole language theory *is* more recent—and problematic—for five reasons:

1. Whole language is the current educational buzzword. Fortunately, this is one buzzword (or two buzzwords?) that reflects sound theory, research, and teaching practice. Unfortunately, many textbook companies, knowing that most school districts are inclined to purchase all-inclusive reading programs, have published what they refer to as "whole language basals," which may contain good literature but have not changed essentially incorrect premises about literacy learning (already detailed in chapter 12). The leopard never really changes its spots! "Whole language basal" is a contradiction in terms.

2. Most schools willing to buy basals and workbooks year after year are unwilling to purchase the many, many children's books necessary for each individual

classroom. Often you will find that good children's literature in a classroom has been scrounged or may even have been purchased by the teacher.

3. Many schools giving lip service to whole language often continue to believe in "skill, drill, and kill." This belief (also detailed in chapter 12) follows the thinking that reading skills are learned in isolated, sequential steps and are usually best practiced through repeated workbook/skill sheet exercise pages. This notion of combining whole language theory/practice with skill-based teaching is like dieting by buying the necessary carrot sticks but dipping them in chocolate sauce.

4. Schools frequently say that they have implemented "parts" of whole language, which usually means that they have purchased enlarged books ("big books"), adopted a "whole language basal," and/or selected a set of books that every child in the school, depending on their grade level, must read. However, little has really changed if schools maintain their former beliefs about literacy development. By merely shifting the literature, not enough has changed.

5. The teachers who utilize whole language strategies that are compatible with whole language theory are at varying stages of understanding that theory. Consequently, practical implementation in the classroom reflects each teacher's level of understanding about whole language. Like parents, most teachers in North America are products of a society schooled in the belief that learning to read is a matter of learning one letter and one skill at a time and gradually increasing the difficulty of the skill. It is not easy for parents or

teachers to rethink a belief system and to change practices that are so deeply ingrained.

The bottom line is that classroom teachers who refer to themselves as whole language teachers are in various stages of understanding and implementation. While I have seen some marvelous teachers who understand both whole language theory and practice, I am respectfully cautious of labeling any classroom a whole language environment simply because the teacher or school says it is.

Q. *I've read all of Danielle Steele's novels, and I'm tired of frivolous vacation reading. I want something to read with meat that will tell me everything I ever wanted to know about whole language and reading theory—but was afraid to ask.*

A. There are two books that come to mind. Ken Goodman's *What's Whole in Whole Language* offers a simple yet complete understanding of the subject matter. Frank Smith's *Reading Without Nonsense* doesn't address whole language per se, but does address the theoretical orientation that became whole language.

Q. *As long as you're recommending books for parents about reading, what are some other suggestions?*

A. Since you've already bought this book, I'd be glad to. *Home: Where Reading and Writing Begin* by Mary Hill and *Reading Begins at Home* by Marie Clay and Dorothy Butler both help parents further understand their role in their child's literacy. In each chapter of *Learning to Read,* Margaret Meek explains a different stage of learning to read and answers questions that parents have about reading.

Q. *Then will all this change in another ten years? Will education be on to another fad after whole language dies?*

A. It's hard to say. It's easy for schools to switch programs once a year, once every five years, or once every ten years. A program concerns itself with how children are taught. Whole language concerns itself with how children *learn*. Methods of instruction change as often as the wind does. *How children learn does not change.* But I can already see some school districts, having taken only small steps toward a whole language philosophy, frightened, shifting back to textbooks that remind me of the materials I used in elementary school. Yuck!

It is my hope that whole language is not a trend and will have staying power. That will ultimately depend on the schools' commitment to current literacy research. But more important, it will depend on administrators and teachers going beyond "programs" and busywork in order to facilitate how children truly learn.

FIFTEEN
A Final Thought

Wendell Phillips, the nineteenth-century abolitionist, said, "You view history not with the eyes but with your prejudices." The same can be said for how we think children learn to read—with our prejudices.

Our prejudices cause many parents to believe that little in their regular daily routines with their child leads to literacy. Our prejudices cause parents to respond to a teacher's request to read every night to their child: "But I do that already; I want to do something really helpful!" Our prejudices cause many parents to find supplemental reading material because they think the teacher spends too much time reading aloud to children and not enough time "teaching reading." Our prejudices cause us to believe that the more sounds a child masters, the better a reader that child will become. And finally, our prejudices lead us to believe that growth is measured by the number of papers a child brings home to show us.

This book's basic message can be summarized with three statements: *talk to your child, provide experiences for your child,* and *read aloud to your child.* As simple as this sounds, it is the essential foundation for literacy. This has always been true about reading. What is different in this decade is that modern educational research has finally justified what good parents have done for so many years. Fortunately, this research is finding its way into classroom methodology.

While parents can sometimes find changes in classroom teaching techniques threatening ("They didn't teach that way when *I* was in school!") and become puzzled over methods unfamiliar to them, no one really expects education to remain stagnant. Learning to read should be easy and natural. It *is* easy and natural when it makes sense, is relevant and interesting to the reader.

Josh is twelve years old now. He is a verbal seventh-grader and a fabulous reader. Josh knows books so well that from time to time he even talks like one.

Josh was in my kindergarten classroom. I remember him beginning to read sometime around January—no thanks to me. I could have handed him the telephone book and he would have learned. But at the time, I took the credit.

Josh gives me the credit as well. I have remained friendly with his family and asked Josh to provide a good quote to complete this book. Something that would sum up everything I have said but in the words of a child. It would make for a nice ending. But Josh is too bright to come up with the spontaneously simple words that I was seeking. He has recently finished reading Tom Clancy's *The Hunt for Red October* and wants to credit me by saying something esoteric like "From my beginnings with a simple book such as *In a Dark, Dark Wood* I have progressed through various levels of books and have now finished a great piece of literature called *Interview With a Vampire*, all thanks to my teacher, Steve."

It's a little much. But I do appreciate the credit. Before I get a swelled head, however, I must put Josh's learning into perspective. My greatest role was *not* to interfere with Josh's own natural emergence into literacy.

But the real credit must go to his mother and father. *They* spent the endless hours reading books to him. *They* suffered through 247 rereadings of *The Very Hungry Caterpillar*. *They* stumbled over all of the books Josh left on the living room floor. *They* put up with a bookshelf that was in a perpetual state of disarray. *They* talked with him. *They* did things with him.

They made my teaching job very easy. I just didn't get in his way.

Special Books for Kids

I have a three-year-old who won't sit still for anything I try to read.

Try moveable books. Eric Hill's Spot books (*Where's Spot?, Spot's First Walk,* and others) are loads of fun. Richard Fowler's lift-the-flap books are full of information. *Mr. Little's Noisy Plane, Mr. Little's Noisy Car,* and *Mr. Little's Noisy* several-other-modes-of-transportation books are fun too, have great illustrations, and very big print. David Carter's *How Many Bugs in a Box?* and its sequel *More Bugs in a Box* are moveable books that have never failed to capture the attention of even the most moveable kid. Eric Carle's many books either move, flip, or have texture (these include *The Very Hungry Caterpillar; The Grouchy Ladybug; The Very Busy Spider; Papa, Please Get the Moon for Me; The Very Quiet Cricket* plus many, many others).

I'm looking for two or three of the best books to give a first-grader for a birthday gift.

This is the answer that is bound to get me into trouble. (I know, I know—there are all kinds of other "best books" available.) These aren't the "best books" as much as three of my favorite birthday gifts to young children. No first-grader should be without *Hattie and the Fox* or *One Hunter*. *The Elephant and the Bad Baby* is repetitive, cumulative, and funny. It is a hit with just about every first-grade child I know.

On a cold, wintry evening I love to snuggle up with my child and read a cozy bedtime book.

The universal bedtime story is *Goodnight, Moon*. Even older children remember it fondly. *Ten, Nine, Eight* is a counting book, just perfect for the parent who wants a warm story to read that will last no longer than a minute. *Go to Sleep, Nicholas Joe* tells about a boy who flies through the night putting children and adults to bed. *Wynken, Blynken, and Nod* is Eugene Field's bedtime poem, imaginatively illustrated by Susan Jeffers. *Winnifred's New Bed* has a cumulative text, each page describing how Winnifred's very big bed gets cozier and cozier. Let your child dreamily fall asleep to Malvina Reynolds's song, *Morningtown Ride*.

You haven't mentioned wordless books. Are they obsolete?

Heavens, no. Wordless books are wonderful books to have in your collection. *Deep in the Forest* tells the Goldilocks and the Three Bears story in reverse. In this version it is Little Bear who visits Goldilocks's family. *The Bear and the Fly* is a hilarious wordless tale of one bear's failed attempts to rid the house of a pesty fly. Instead he swats and knocks everyone in the family unconscious. *Changes, Changes* offers lots of opportunity to discuss the various transformations that two wooden figures make of a group of blocks. *The Snowman* tells of a little boy who builds a snowman that comes to life. *The Grey Lady and the Strawberry Snatcher* is an eerie tale of a green creature with a purple hat that follows the grey lady to the swamp. *The Knight and the Dragon*—a very funny story about an inexperienced knight and an equally inexperienced dragon—is nearly wordless.

My child loves factual information, but most books seem to be too sophisticated for his age.

Obviously you haven't seen any of Gail Gibbons's books. I can't think of anybody who does a better job with showing how things work with both words and clear illustrations. *The Milk Makers, Up Goes the Skyscraper,* and *The Puffins Are Back* are only three of many titles that describe exactly the subject matter of each book. Kathryn Lasky's *Puppeteer* explains the workings of a string puppet, and *Sugaring Time,* through photographs, illustrates how maple sugar and syrup come from trees. Look for Ruth Heller's rich and absorbing books about a variety of subjects: *Chickens Aren't the Only Ones, The Reason for a Flower, Animals Born Alive and Well, Plants That Never Ever Bloom. Snakes Are Hunters* is one of a series of science books with interesting text and authentic illustrations. Russell Freedman's *Sharks* has as absorbing photography as narrative. Older children love the humor of Joanna Cole's Magic School Bus series, as the bus travels inside the earth, into the reservoir system and through the waterworks, and then to outer space. Children should not be relegated to reading only the encyclopedia.

Keep in mind that many works of fiction include factual information too. What better book about spiders than *Charlotte's Web!*

My child has a bad case of things-that-go-bump-in-the-night syndrome. Are there a couple of bedtime stories that will help lessen his fears?

I'm not convinced that bibliotherapy really helps, but we all try it in the hopes that it will. Two of my favorites are *A World Full of Monsters* and *There's a Nightmare in My Closet. Monsters* offers a reassuring explanation of the history of monsters and how to handle the bedroom noise that monsters make by night. *Nightmare* is about a little boy who uses a pop gun to overcome a nightmare hiding in his closet, but who is then joined by the monster who fears yet another monster in the closet.

Are there children's illustrators whose books you would buy sight unseen?

Tomie dePaola is an incredibly prolific and wonderful artist. (And I'm not just saying this because of his warm foreword to this book.) His illustrations are bright, colorful, optimistic, and have a distinct style. I will never forget watching him teach a group of 300 teachers how to draw Strega Nona. He used an overhead projector, and was asked to photocopy the transparency for all the teachers. Characteristically, he signed all 300 photocopies. Jan Brett's illustrations are always rich and exquisitely detailed. Her trademark borders surround each illustration. Like Tomie, she gravitates toward folklore. And I have never seen a warmer, kinder, more thoughtful person respond to children's requests for autographed books. Audrey and Don Wood always have a lush tale to tell. I can look at their meticulous illustrations over and over without ever growing tired of them.

I miss the classics. I want to read my child a book that has been around for years and years.

Where the Wild Things Are will outlast all of us. *Charlotte's Web* takes on new meaning with each new stage of my life. I will be forever in awe of the imagination of L. Frank Baum's *The Wizard of Oz. Alice's Adventures in Wonderland* and *Through the Looking Glass* age like fine wine.

My child hates poetry. How will she ever enjoy Emily Dickinson?

Start her with just about anything by Jack Prelutsky. The man is wonderfully funny. His collections are too numerous to list but I must mention *New Kid on the Block* and *Something Big Has Been Here.* Both are large collections of his poetry, appreciated as much by adults as by children. Karla Kuskin is one of our finest children's poets. While Prelutsky writes exclusively with rhythm and rhyme, Karla Kuskin's poetry seldom rhymes. *Dogs and Dragons, Trees and Dreams* is one example of Karla's many books. In this anthology, she describes many of her poems, sometimes pointing out the sounds of words, rhythm, patterns, or moods. Eloise Greenfield writes from the contemporary African-American experience in *Nathaniel Talking,* poetry of rap and rhyme, and *Honey, I Love,* a collection of love poems.

You can't ignore letters altogether. Do you have a few favorite alphabet books?

Absolutely. Believe it or not, one of my favorites is *A Peaceable Kingdom: The Shaker ABECEDARIUS*, which can actually be sung to the tune of "Little Brown Jug." (Don't ever accuse me of being too progressive!) *Alligator Arrived with Apples* and *Hosie's Alphabet* are alliterative feasts. *Q Is for Duck* is wonderfully imaginative (A is for Zoo. Why? Because . . . Animals live in the Zoo. B is for Dog. Why? Because a Dog Barks.)

My child is fascinated by mathematics. Are there any books he'd enjoy?

There are literally hundreds of titles that discuss a variety of mathematical ideas. *One Crow* is a counting book in which each rhyming verse introduces another barnyard animal. Similar counting patterns include *One Bear All Alone, Ten Black Dots, The Twelve Days of Christmas,* and *Roll Over.* Classification is pictured through photography in Tana Hoban's *Is It Red? Is It Yellow? Is It Blue?* as well as in her *Is It Rough? Is It Smooth? Is It Shiny?* David Schwartz writes about the conceptualization of a million, billion, and trillion in *How Much Is a Million?* Mitsumasa Anno and son Masaichiro Anno offer simple pictures to introduce the fascinating and complex concepts of factorials in *Anno's Mysterious Multiplying Jar.*

A book with chapters for a six-year-old?

Most beginning readers love to hear novels—and they should. *Charlie and the Chocolate Factory,* and *James and the Giant Peach* are favorites. I think that *Jacob Two-*

Two and the Hooded Fang is full of fanciful adventure. Beverly Cleary's Ramona books are much loved. *How to Eat Fried Worms* is a riot and captures the attention of many young children. Young kids appreciate Judy Blume's *Tales of a Fourth Grade Nothing,* the saga of how nine-year-old Peter Hatcher survives with two-year-old Fudge. Sequels *Superfudge* and *Fudge-A-Mania* are also favorites. Finally, my personal favorite as a young child was *Mr. Popper's Penguins,* the story of a kindly housepainter who brings into his home an entire flock of penguins.

Our daughter is just starting to read on her own. What books would you suggest?

Harper and Row publish a series of I Can Read books that provide fun and entertaining stories for beginning independent readers. My three favorites include *Frog and Toad Together, Little Bear,* and *Mouse Tales. Frog and Toad Together* is one of four books about these two best friends who share activities and adventures. *Little Bear* is one of five books about the warm relationship between Little Bear, his friends, and family. *Mouse Tales* includes Papa Mouse telling seven short bedtime stories, which are funny and wonderful. Literal and non-literal children adore eleven different *Amelia Bedelia* books, the housekeeper who really does "dress" the chicken and "separate" the eggs.

I can't sit and read to my child twenty-four hours a day, yet he can never get his fill of books. Any ideas?

While they'll never replace you, try some of the books taped for children. My favorites are published by Knopf with celebrities as narrators: Jack Nicholson reads *The*

Elephant's Child, Cher reads *The Ugly Duckling,* Judy Collins reads *Thumbelina,* and Meryl Streep reads *The Velveteen Rabbit.*

I have a screaming six-month-old, and I can't find the time to get to a bookstore. Is there any way of accessing good books from a sitting position?

I've had much luck with Chinaberry Book Service, a mail order children's book service. Their highly imaginative, descriptive catalog is sent to homes throughout the United States, Canada, and anywhere in the world. Their service is prompt, and for an additional fee books can be sent within two days. They'll even gift wrap! Aside from being a good service for parents, they stock only the best quality children's books. Their toll-free number (at printing) is 800-776-2242.

I need a complete summary of children's books. Can you suggest any resources?

No bibliography is ever complete since so many wonderful new books come into print each year. However, many parents have found *The New York Times Parent's Guide to the Best Books for Children* a particularly useful summary. Each book is succinctly described and includes the author, illustrator, publisher, and publishing date. It is also nicely classified into six categories: wordless books, picture books, story books, early reading books, middle reading books, and young adult books. Jim Trelease's *Read-Aloud Handbook* is a valuable resource for read-alouds and includes many handy read-aloud strategies. *The Horn Book Magazine,* published six times a year, includes reviews of new children's books as well as frequent reminders of old favorites. I use this resource to stay current with the onslaught of so many books. *The Horn Book* also publishes *The Horn Book Guide to Children's and Young Adult Books*, which comes out twice a year in March and September. Their toll-free number (again, at printing) is 800-325-1170 (U.S. only). I also recommend *For Love of Reading*, a book published by Consumer Reports. The authors have interesting comments about children at various ages and suggest age-appropriate books. They also include a lengthy children's book bibliography and a list of resources for parents that every over-involved mom and dad will have a field day with.

Quite frankly, while all of these books have good bibliographies, these can be overwhelming. They are usually a too-lengthy list of books, which I refer to only to confirm what I already know. I include this book's bibliography in that description as well. Because of this, I hope you will read this book first and use the references only as a means of finding the book or books in which you are interested. (See Select Bibliography, page 155.)

Select Bibliography

Children's books go in and out of print rather quickly, so, while most of the books listed here are currently in print, there is no guarantee that they will remain so. Also, some of the books are available in "library edition" only. This means your bookstore may not order them for you as their discount is too small to make ordering profitable. Nag them anyway. Remember also that you can't possibly own every good book; libraries are important sources of books, in and out of print. Most librarians are both helpful and knowledgeable. Make use of them. Some of my best friends, thankfully, are librarians!

This bibliography includes only those books that have been referred to in this book.

Aliki. *Go Tell Aunt Rhody*. New York: Macmillan, 1974.

Anno, Masaichiro, and Mitsumasa Anno. *Anno's Mysterious Multiplying Jar*. New York: Philomel, 1983.

Atwater, Richard, and Florence Atwater. *Mr. Popper's Penguins*. New York: Little, Brown, 1938.

Aylesworth, Jim. *One Crow: A Counting Rhyme*. New York: J. B. Lippincott, 1988.

Bang, Molly. *Ten, Nine, Eight*. New York: Greenwillow, 1983.

————. *The Grey Lady and the Strawberry Snatcher*. New York: Four Winds Press, 1980.

Baskin, Hosea, et al. (illustrations by Leonard Baskin). *Hosie's Alphabet*. New York: Viking Press, 1972.

Baum, Frank L. (illustrations by Michael Hague). *The Wizard of Oz*. New York: Knopf, 1982.

Beck, Ian. *Little Miss Muffet*. Oxford: Oxford University Press, 1988.

Blume, Judy. *Tales of a Fourth Grade Nothing*. New York: Dutton, 1972.

————. *Superfudge*. New York: Dutton, 1980.

————. *Fudge-A-Mania*. New York: Dutton, 1990.

Brett, Jan. *The Twelve Days of Christmas*. New York: Putnam, 1986.

Briggs, Raymond. *The Snowman*. New York: Random House, 1978.

Brown, Margaret Wise. *Goodnight, Moon*. New York: Harper, 1947.

Bucknall, Caroline. *One Bear All Alone*. New York: Dial Books for Young Readers, 1985.

Butler, Dorothy, and Marie Clay. *Reading Begins at Home*. Portsmouth, NH: Heinemann, 1987.

Carle, Eric. *Papa, Please Get the Moon for Me*. Saxonville, MA: Picture Book Studio, 1986.

————. *The Grouchy Ladybug*. New York: T. Y. Crowell, 1977.

————. *The Very Busy Spider*. New York: Philomel, 1984.

————. *The Very Hungry Caterpillar*. New York: Philomel, 1969.

————. *The Very Quiet Cricket*. New York: Philomel, 1990.

Carroll, Lewis (illustrations by Michael Hague). *Alice's Adventures in Wonderland*. New York: Knopf, 1982.

————. (illustrations by S. Michelle Wiggins). *Through the Looking Glass*. New York: Holt, Rinehart and Winston, 1986.

Carter, David. *How Many Bugs in a Box?* New York: Little Simon, 1988.

————. *More Bugs in a Box*. New York: Simon and Schuster Books for Young Readers, 1990.

Cauley, Lorinda (author/illustrator). *Three Blind Mice*. New York: Putnam, 1991.

Charlip, Remy. *Fortunately*. New York: Macmillan, 1964.

Chartier, Normand (author/illustrator). *Over the River and Thro' the Woods*. New York: Little Simon, 1987.

Cleary, Beverly. *Ramona the Pest*. New York: William Morrow, 1968.

Cole, Joanna. *The Magic School Bus at the Waterworks*. New York: Scholastic, 1986.

———. *The Magic School Bus: Lost in Outer Space*. New York: Scholastic, 1990.

———. *The Magic School Bus: Inside the Earth*. New York: Scholastic, 1987.

Crews, Donald. *Ten Black Dots*. New York: Greenwillow, 1968, 1986 (rev.).

Dahl, Roald. *James and the Giant Peach*. New York: Knopf, 1961.

———. *Charlie and the Chocolate Factory*. New York: Knopf, 1964.

Degan, Bruce (author/illustrator). *Jamberry*. New York: Harper and Row, 1983.

dePaola, Tomie. *The Knight and the Dragon*. Putnam, 1980.

Dragonwagon, Crescent. *Alligator Arrived with Apples: A Potluck Alphabet Feast*. New York: Macmillan, 1987.

Elting, Mary, and Michael Folsom. *Q Is for Duck: An Alphabet Guessing Game*. New York: Clarion, 1980.

Field, Eugene (illustrations by Susan Jeffers). *Wynken, Blynken, and Nod*. New York: Dutton, 1982.

Fowke, Edith (illustrations by Merle Peek). *Roll Over! A Counting Song*. New York: Clarion, 1981.

Fowler, Richard. *Mr. Little's Noisy Car*. New York: Grosset and Dunlap, 1985.

———. *Mr. Little's Noisy Plane*. New York: Grosset and Dunlap, 1988.

Fox, Mem. *Hattie and the Fox.* New York: Bradbury Press, 1986.

Freedman, Russell. *Sharks.* New York: Holiday House, 1985.

Frost, Robert (illustrations by Susan Jeffers). *Stopping by Woods on a Snowy Evening.* New York: Dutton, 1978.

Galdone, Paul. *Over in the Meadow.* New York: Prentice-Hall Books for Young Readers, 1986.

———. *The Little Red Hen.* New York: Scholastic, 1973.

———.*The Three Little Pigs.* New York: Clarion, 1970.

Gibbons, Gail. *The Milk Makers.* New York: Macmillan, 1985.

———. *Up Goes the Skyscraper.* New York: Four Winds, 1986.

———. *The Puffins Are Back.* New York: HarperCollins, 1991.

Ginsburg, Mirra (trans. from the Russian). *The Chick and the Duckling* by V. Suteyev. New York: Macmillan, 1972.

———. *Where Does the Sun Go at Night?* adapted from an Armenian song. New York: Greenwillow, 1981.

Goodman, Ken. *What's Whole in Whole Language.* Portsmouth, NH: Heinemann, 1986.

Greenfield, Eloise. *Honey, I Love and Other Love Poems.* New York: T. Y. Crowell/HarperCollins, 1978.

———. *Nathaniel Talking.* New York: Black Butterfly Children's Books, 1988.

Hale, Sarah (illustrations by Tomie dePaola). *Mary Had a Little Lamb.* New York: Holiday House, 1984.

Hawkins, Colin, and Jacqui Hawkins. *Old Mother Hubbard.* New York: Putnam, 1985.

Heilbroner, Joan. *This Is the House Where Jack Lives.* New York: Harper and Row, 1962.

Heller, Ruth. *Chickens Aren't the Only Ones.* New York: Grosset and Dunlap, 1981.

———. *Animals Born Alive and Well.* New York: Grosset and Dunlap, 1982.

———. *The Reason for a Flower.* New York: Grosset and Dunlap, 1983.

Hill, Eric. *Spot's First Walk*. New York: Putnam, 1981.

———. *Where's Spot?* New York: Putnam, 1980.

Hill, Mary. *Where Reading and Writing Begin*. Portsmouth, NH: Heinemann, 1989.

Hoban, Tana. *Is It Red? Is It Yellow? Is It Blue? An Adventure in Color*. New York: Greenwillow, 1978.

———. *Is It Rough? Is It Smooth? Is It Shiny?* New York: Greenwillow, 1984.

Howell, Richard, and Lynn Howell. *Winnifred's New Bed*. New York: Alfred A. Knopf, 1985.

Hutchins, Pat. *Changes, Changes*. New York: Macmillan, 1971.

———. *One Hunter*. New York: Greenwillow, 1982.

———. *Rosie's Walk*. New York: Macmillan, 1968.

Ivimey, John (illustrations by Paul Galdone). *Three Blind Mice*. New York: Clarion, 1987.

Kalan, Robert. *Rain*. New York: Greenwillow, 1978.

Kipling, Rudyard (illustrations by Tim Raglin). *The Elephant's Child*. New York: Random House, 1986.

Kosza, Keiko. *When the Elephant Walks*. New York: Putnam, 1990.

Kraus, Robert. *Whose Mouse Are You?* New York: Macmillan, 1970.

Kuskin, Karla. *Dogs and Dragons, Trees and Dreams: A Collection of Poems*. New York: Harper and Row, 1980.

Lasky, Kathryn. *Puppeteer*. New York: Macmillan, 1985.

———. *Sugaring Time*. New York: Macmillan, 1983.

Lauber, Patricia. *Snakes Are Hunters*. New York: Thomas Cromwell, 1988.

Lear, Edward (illustrations by Jan Brett). *The Owl and the Pussycat*. New York: Philomel, 1991.

Lipson, Eden. *Parent's Guide to the Best Books for Children*. New York: New York Times Parent's Guide, 1988.

Lobel, Arnold. *Frog and Toad Together*. New York: HarperCollins (I Can Read), 1972.

Martin Jr., Bill. *Brown Bear, Brown Bear, What Do You See?* New York: Holt, Rinehart and Winston, 1967.

Mayer, Mercer. *There's a Nightmare in My Closet.* New York: Dial Books for Young Readers, 1968.

McQueen, John. *A World Full of Monsters.* New York: Crowell, 1986.

Meek, Margaret. *Learning to Read.* London: The Bodley Head, 1982.

Minarik, Else (illustrations by Maurice Sendak). *Little Bear.* New York: HarperCollins (I Can Read), 1957.

Nichol, bp. *Once: A Lullaby.* New York: Greenwillow, 1983.

O'Donnell, Elizabeth. *The Twelve Days of Summer.* New York: Morrow Junior Books, 1991.

Parish, Peggy. *Amelia Bedelia.* New York: Harper and Row, 1963.

Pearson, Tracey (author/illustrator). *Sing a Song of Sixpence.* New York: Dial Books for Young Readers, 1985.

Prelutsky, Jack. *New Kid on the Block.* New York: Greenwillow, 1984.

———. *Something Big Has Been Here.* New York: Greenwillow, 1990.

Provensen, Alice, and Martin Provensen. *A Peaceable Kingdom: The Shaker ABECEDARIUS.* New York: Viking, 1978.

Raffi (illustrations by David Allender). *Shake My Sillies Out: Raffi Songs to Read.* New York: Crown, 1987.

———. (illustrations by Nadine Westcott). *Down By the Bay: Raffi Songs to Read.* New York: Crown, 1987.

Rees, Mary. *Ten in a Bed.* Boston: Joy Street Books, 1988.

Reynolds, Malvina (illustrations by Michael Leeman). *Morningtown Ride.* Roseville, CA: Turn the Page Press, 1984.

Rockwell, Thomas. *How to Eat Fried Worms.* New York: Franklin Watts, 1973.

Rudman, Marsha, Anna Pearce, et al. *For Love of Reading: A Parent's Guide to Encouraging Readers from Infancy Through Age 5*. Mount Vernon: Consumers Union, 1985.

Schwartz, David. *How Much Is a Million?* New York: Lothrop, Lee and Shepard Books, 1985.

Sendak, Maurice. *Where the Wild Things Are*. New York: Harper and Row, 1963.

Shannon, George. *Lizard's Song*. New York: Greenwillow, 1981.

———. *Dance Away*. New York: Greenwillow, 1982.

Sharmat, Marjorie. *Go to Sleep, Nicholas Joe*. New York: Harper and Row, 1988.

Trelease, Jim. *The Read-Aloud Handbook*. New York: Penguin, revised 1985.

Turkle, Brinton. *Deep in the Forest*. New York: Dutton, 1976.

Vipont, Elfreida, and Raymond Briggs. *The Elephant and the Bad Baby*. New York: Coward-McCann, 1969.

Weatherill, Stephen (author/illustrator). *Humpty Dumpty*. New York: Greenwillow, 1982.

Westcott, Nadine. *The House That Jack Built*. Boston: Joy Street Books, 1991.

Williams, Linda. *The Little Old Lady Who Was Not Afraid of Anything*. New York: Crowell, 1986.

Wildsmith, Brian (author/illustrator). *Cat on the Mat*. Oxford: Oxford University Press, 1982.

Winter, Paula. *The Bear and the Fly: A Story*. New York: Crown, 1976.

Wood, Audrey (illustrations by Don Wood). *The Napping House*. New York: Harcourt Brace Jovanovich, 1984.

Yektai, Niki. *Bears in Pairs*. New York: Bradbury, 1987.

Zemach, Harve. *The Judge: An Untrue Tale*. New York: Farrar, Straus and Giroux, 1969.